DEVELOPMENT CENTI

D0832311

AGRICULTURAL TRADE LIBERALISATION AND INDIA

by
Shankar Subramanian

HD
9016
.I42S82
1993

DEVELOPMENT CENTRE
OF THE ORGANISATION FOR ECONOMIC CO-OPERATION AND DEVELOPMENT

ORGANISATION FOR ECONOMIC CO-OPERATION AND DEVELOPMENT

Pursuant to Article 1 of the Convention signed in Paris on 14th December 1960, and which came into force on 30th September 1961, the Organisation for Economic Co-operation and Development (OECD) shall promote policies designed:

— to achieve the highest sustainable economic growth and employment and a rising standard of living in Member countries, while maintaining financial stability, and thus to contribute to the development of the world economy;

— to contribute to sound economic expansion in Member as well as non-member countries in the process of economic development; and

— to contribute to the expansion of world trade on a multilateral, non-discriminatory basis in accordance with international obligations.

The original Member countries of the OECD are Austria, Belgium, Canada, Denmark, France, Germany, Greece, Iceland, Ireland, Italy, Luxembourg, the Netherlands, Norway, Portugal, Spain, Sweden, Switzerland, Turkey, the United Kingdom and the United States. The following countries became Members subsequently through accession at the dates indicated hereafter: Japan (28th April 1964), Finland (28th January 1969), Australia (7th June 1971) and New Zealand (29th May 1973). The Commission of the European Communities takes part in the work of the OECD (Article 13 of the OECD Convention).

The Development Centre of the Organisation for Economic Co-operation and Development was established by decision of the OECD Council on 23rd October 1962.

The purpose of the Centre is to bring together the knowledge and experience available in Member countries of both economic development and the formulation and execution of general economic policies; to adapt such knowledge and experience to the actual needs of countries or regions in the process of development and to put the results at the disposal of the countries by appropriate means.

The Centre has a special and autonomous position within the OECD which enables it to enjoy scientific independence in the execution of its task. Nevertheless, the Centre can draw upon the experience and knowledge available in the OECD in the development field.

Publié en français sous le titre :

LA LIBÉRALISATION DES ÉCHANGES AGRICOLES
ET L'INDE

THE OPINIONS EXPRESSED AND ARGUMENTS EMPLOYED IN THIS PUBLICATION ARE THE SOLE RESPONSIBILITY OF THE AUTHOR AND DO NOT NECESSARILY REFLECT THOSE OF THE OECD OR OF THE GOVERNMENTS OF ITS MEMBER COUNTRIES

*
* *

© OECD 1993
Applications for permission to reproduce or translate all or part of this publication should be made to:
Head of Publications Service, OECD
2, rue André-Pascal, 75775 PARIS CEDEX 16, France

Foreword

This book is one in a series of case studies commissioned in the context of the 1990-92 work programme of the OECD Development Centre on "Developing Country Agriculture and International Economic Trends" under the direction of Ian Goldin.

ALSO AVAILABLE

Agricultural Trade Liberalization. Implications for Developing Countries *edited by Ian Goldin, Odin Knudsen.* Series Development Centre Seminars (1990)
(41 90 04 1) ISBN 92-64-13366-6　　　　　　　　　　　FF180　£18.00　US$32.95　DM60

Agriculture and Economic Crisis. Lessons from Brazil *by Ian Goldin, Gervasio Castro de Rezende.* Series Development Centre Studies (1990)
(41 89 09 1) ISBN 92-64-13392-5　　　　　　　　　　　FF90　£11.00　US$19.00　DM35

The Future of Agriculture: Developing Country Implications *by Martin Brown, Ian Goldin.* Series Development Centre Studies (1992)
(41 92 02 1) ISBN 92-64-13628-2　　　　　　　　　　　FF160　£20.00　US$38.00　DM62

Investing in Food *by Ruth Rama.* Series Development Centre Studies (1992)
(41 92 08 1) ISBN 92-64-13747-5　　　　　　　　　　　FF220　£32.00　US$55.00　DM90

Prices charged at the OECD Bookshop.

THE OECD CATALOGUE OF PUBLICATIONS and supplements will be sent free of charge on request addressed either to OECD Publications Service, or to the OECD Distributor in your country.

Table of Contents

Acknowledgements   7
Preface   9
Executive Summary   11
Introduction   17

Chapter 1.   **A Review of Indian Agricultural Performance**   19

1. Agricultural Growth.   19
2. Regional Differences   20
3. Government Intervention and Producer Incentives   22
4. The Public Distribution System   25
5. Intervention in External Trade.   26
Notes and References.   27

Chapter 2.   **The Social Accounting Matrix and the Model**   29

1. The Social Accounting Matrix   29
2. The Model   30
Notes and References.   38

Chapter 3.   **Scenarios for Policy Reforms**   41

1. Agricultural Liberalisation in India.   44
2. Liberalisation of Trade in all Commodities   46
3. Liberalisation of World Agricultural Trade   47
4. Technical Change.   49
5. Cutting Fertilizer Subsidies   52
6. Food Subsidy Policy   54
7. Summary of Results.   56
Notes and References.   59

Chapter 4.   **Conclusion**   63

Appendix 1. **Building a SAM for India**   67
Appendix 2. **The Model**   71
Appendix 3. **The Equations of the Model**   75

Bibliography   85

List of Tables

Table 1   Pre- and Post-green Revolution Period Growth Rates in Crop Production, Crop Area and Yield. All India   87

Table 2   Pre- and Post-green Revolution Period Growth Rates in Crop Production, Area and Yield. All India (Adjusted for Variations in Rainfall)   87

Table 3   Composition of Regions and Regional Shares in Foodgrain Production, 1988/89   88

Table 4   Regional Foodgrain Yields and Area and Input Shares (1980 and 1988)   89

Table 5   Regional Growth Rates of Area, Production and Yield, 1952/53-1988/89 . . .   90

Table 6   Marketed Surplus as Fraction of Production (Various Years) and Share of Production (1988-89)   91

Table 7   Input Structure of Wheat and Rice (Average of 1981-82 to 1983-84)   92

Table 8   Labour Absorption for Major Crops and States   94

Table 9   Unit Costs, Support Prices and Market Prices in High and Low Productivity Regions, Wheat and Rice   95

Table 10   Subsidies on Wheat and Rice   96

Table 11   Social Accounting Matrix for India   97

Table 12   Household Incomes, Savings and Sources of Income   100

Table 13   Agricultural Supply and Input Demand Elasticities   101

Table 14   Structure of Trade and Production (1983-84)   102

Table 15   Scenarios 1 & 2: Trade Liberalisation in India   103

Table 16   Scenario 3: Liberalisation of World Agricultural Trade   106

Table 17   Scenario 4: 10% Increase in Yields   109

Table 18   Scenario 5: 80% Reduction in Fertilizer Subsidy   112

Table 19   Scenarios 6 & 7: Food Subsidy Policy   115

Acknowledgements

The OECD Development Centre and the author gratefully acknowledge the financial support of the Finnish and Swiss Governments for the Development Centre's country studies, and the assistance of the Rockefeller Foundation in facilitating the Bellagio meeting in which the project's findings were reviewed. The author thanks participants at the meeting and Hans Binswanger, Ian Goldin, Alain de Janvry, Sherman Robinson, Elisabeth Sadoulet, K. Subbarao and Dominique van der Mensbrugghe for their comments on earlier drafts, and is grateful to Ashok Gulati for helpful advice and for providing copies of his recent work. The opinions expressed in this study are the sole responsibility of the author and do not necessarily reflect those of the OECD, nor any other institution or individual.

Preface

Structural adjustment and trade liberalisation are matters of immediate and deep concern for all those interested in economic development. Research carried out within the OECD Development Centre's programme on "Developing Country Agriculture and International Economic Trends" aims to provide fresh perspectives which may facilitate the economic reform process.

The Centre's research on agriculture incorporates several components: a conceptual component to provide analytical guidance for the broader issues; a global general equilibrium model to analyse the overall trends and policy consequences; a component to analyse the links between economic reform and technological change in agriculture; and a series of country case studies, of which this is one, to look at the reform options and their implications for individual representative countries. This study provides analytical insights into the interactions between macroeconomic and trade policies and agricultural development in India.

The size of its population and the scale of its economy mean that Indian policies inevitably have repercussions for global human and economic development. India's political non-alignment has translated into heterodox independence in its economic policies which until recently provided a remarkable basis for growth. The slowing of this growth nevertheless has prompted a reconsideration of economic policies. At the heart of the current debate lies the question of trade liberalisation and its relationship to macroeconomic and agricultural sector reform. Despite rapid industrial development, agriculture remains the major sector, and three-quarters of the population — some 640 million people — live in the countryside.

The reform process underway aims to secure high rates of sustainable growth, and the policies proposed will serve to alter patterns of production, consumption and trade, with far-reaching implications for income growth and distribution. Given India's size, the repercussions will be felt in international markets and be reflected in changing patterns of trade and prices. This international dimension has been examined by the Development Centre in the context of its global Rural-Urban North-South modelling exercise, while the domestic dimension is being modelled in parallel studies of China, Brazil and Mexico.

In this study Shankar Subramanian uses a computable general equilibrium model to examine the implications of seven alternative reform options. In addition to identifying the potential winners and losers, the analysis provides perspectives on the extent and strength of the linkages between economy-wide and sectoral policies. Thus

9

it is shown that policies aimed at industry are more important to agriculture than agriculture-specific policies, and that these industrial policies serve as an important impediment to agricultural growth.

This modelling effort represents a major methodological advance, yielding policy insights on the sequencing of the reform efforts. Of particular note is the conclusion that despite longer run improvements, the rural and urban poor may be adversely affected in the short run by liberalisation, suggesting that measures designed to offset the adverse effects may be necessary to ensure that liberalisation is not associated with higher levels of poverty and that the policies are sustainable. Targeted food subsidies and technical growth in agriculture is shown to be beneficial to the rural and urban poor.

The study provides a state-of-the-art analysis of two central policy issues: first, how will agricultural and industrial liberalisation affect economic growth and sectoral performance? and, second, what will be the implications for the distribution of incomes of this domestic reform, and its possible coupling with trade reforms undertaken in other countries? The study shows conclusively that agricultural growth serves to alleviate poverty and that liberalised trade can be used to improve agricultural prices and enhance productivity gains. In providing a basis for examining the reforms and their sequencing in a quantitative framework, the study makes a valuable and timely contribution to the debate on policy reform. I trust that it will be of great interest to Indian policy-makers and to a wider audience.

Jean Bonvin
OECD Development Centre
January 1993

Executive Summary

This study begins by reviewing India's recent agricultural performance and the role of state intervention in agriculture and its effects on producer incentives, highlighting the need for policy reform. The study then frames several different scenarios for domestic policy reforms and for a possible major change in the world economic environment — the increase in world agricultural prices that is expected to result from agricultural trade liberalisation by the OECD countries under GATT. A computable general equilibrium model of the Indian economy is used to simulate the outcomes of these scenarios. Keeping in view the institutional context, the results from these simulations are used to provide insights into domestic policy reforms and the implications for India of higher world agricultural prices.

Owing to the sheer size of India's agricultural sector and the importance of agricultural products in the consumer budget, agricultural performance and agricultural policy have an economy-wide impact. In addition, the bulk of the poor are in rural areas and are dependent on agriculture. Consequently, agricultural policy and performance have been major concerns of policy-makers in India. As in most other countries, government intervention in agriculture is extensive. State intervention has produced a complex combination of explicit and implicit subsidies and taxes that differ across crops and regions. Moreover, agriculture-related budgetary subsidies have increased rapidly, reaching a level where they have begun to cause significant macroeconomic strain. Agricultural policy reform has taken on greater urgency after the recent crisis in India's balance of payments, which prompted the government to liberalise exchange controls and trade significantly and to reduce budgetary subsidies.

Agricultural policy reform raises several key issues. First, while trade liberalisation is expected to lead to improved resource allocation and higher output, aggregate welfare may decrease in the short or medium run because of slow reallocation of resources. In addition, some groups may remain losers even in the long run. Secondly, given the prevailing high level of industrial protection, the impact on agriculture of a reduction in industrial protection may be larger than that of complete liberalisation of agricultural trade. Thirdly, while the effects of domestic reforms on growth and distribution are themselves of great importance, these reforms take on added significance in the context of possible world agricultural trade liberalisation. Recent studies have pointed out that liberalisation of world agricultural trade will lead to higher agricultural prices. In the absence of agricultural trade liberalisation by India, price transmission elasticities for agricultural commodities are likely to be small in anything but the long run, so that the increase in world agricultural prices will have little effect. Higher world prices will have much greater impact after India liberalises its agricultural trade, thereby significantly increasing price transmission elasticities.

The main features of India's agricultural performance are well known. After half a century of stagnation, Indian agriculture attained growth rates of between 2.5 per cent and 3 per cent after the 1950s. The seeming lack of change in growth rate during the latter period obscures a significant change in the character of growth. Expansion of sown area was a major source of growth before the mid-1960s. Growth after the mid-1960s was the result largely of increasing yields. Underlying this change was the increasing adoption of the Green Revolution "package" of high-yielding varieties and chemical fertilizers. This new technology was most successful in raising yields of rice and wheat in areas with good water control. As a result, the share of rice and wheat in output has increased while growth rates have fallen for crops which did not benefit as much from the new technology, such as pulses and coarse cereals. In addition, because of large agroclimatic differences across regions and availability and quality of irrigation, among other factors, the differences in yield growth rates across crops have resulted in large differences in agricultural output growth rates across regions. One consequence of these changes is that production, marketed surplus and government purchases of rice and wheat have become increasingly concentrated in the three Northern states of Punjab, Haryana and Uttar Pradesh. A second is that growth has been slow in areas which lack either water or proper water control — often areas with a high incidence of poverty. A third consequence is that large regional variations exist in input use, degree of mechanisation and labour use for the same crop, leading to substantial variations in production costs.

Government intervention in agricultural markets is widespread. Price policy is determined by a combination of controls on foreign trade (which until recently were highly restrictive) and domestic measures, motivated by the desire to improve food security and enhance producer incentives. Food rationing in urban areas began during the Second World War and was continued as food shortages persisted. Until the mid-1960s, domestic procurement was low and the ration system's requirements were met largely through imports, chiefly of wheat from the United States, so that producer taxation through procurement was small. With the advent of the Green Revolution, the rationale of price policy changed. In order to encourage adoption of the new technology, support and procurement prices were set so as to assure a positive return after subtracting returns to capital, land and own labour. Procurement has been essentially limited to rice and wheat. Intervention in domestic markets for other major commodities has not been important (because market prices have remained above support prices) except for cotton and sugar cane, for which prices are set by the government.

Procurement of cereals was effected through a variety of means such as levies on traders and millers, pre-emptive purchases and the use of restrictions on exporting cereals from surplus regions. However, by the late 1970s government cereal stocks had become very large and these restrictions were abandoned. Procurement is now concentrated in the Northern states of Punjab, Haryana and Uttar Pradesh and accounts for a substantial part of the marketed surplus of wheat and rice in these states. Procurement and harvest prices in this region have converged over time and it has been argued that as a result procurement no longer damages producer incentives in these states. Elsewhere, procurement is small and market prices have been high enough to assure the producer a positive return.

From its origins as a scheme for distributing food equitably in urban areas, the ration system has moved toward the objective of transferring income to the poor. However, its success in this regard is questionable. Firstly, coverage of rural areas where most of the poor live is poor. Secondly, many states make no attempt to restrict access to the poor. Thirdly, the distribution of subsidised food across states bears almost no relation to the distribution of poor people. Fourthly, the budgetary cost of the system has increased rapidly because marketing margins have gone up faster than inflation and faster than procurement prices. But it should be noted that the nutritional benefits of rations are found to be substantial in states with extensive rural coverage, suggesting that the ration scheme could be effective if it were targeted and if state agencies' margins were to be contained.

Government intervention also extends to agricultural inputs, such as electricity, fertilizer and irrigation, which are provided by public agencies. While input subsidies were small initially, rapid growth in input use and the inability to pass on increases in costs has resulted in a rapidly increasing subsidy bill, with the subsidies for electricity and fertilizer amounting to some $4.7 billion in 1989-90.

The net effect of interventions in domestic markets and international trade is to cause domestic and world prices to differ. Recent estimates of nominal and effective protection coefficients suggest that rice and cotton are taxed and wheat is neither protected nor taxed, while oilseeds and sugar cane are highly protected. In addition, there are substantial variations in protection rates across regions, stemming from differences in transport costs and input use. Taken with the marked unevenness in commercialisation rates across regions, this suggests that substantial regional variations can be expected in the impact of changes in trade policy or in world prices.

The turn toward economic liberalisation in India has brought agricultural policy reform to the forefront. The outcome of domestic policy reform can be significantly affected by changes in the world economic environment, such as the increase in world agricultural prices which is expected to follow agricultural trade liberalisation by the OECD, countries. Three sets of scenarios are used to examine these possibilities. The first set considers different scenarios for trade liberalisation in India with and without higher world agricultural prices. The second considers domestic policy issues, such as reducing the fertilizer subsidy and different responses to an exogenous increase in agricultural yields, and the third is concerned with food subsidy policy.

The outcomes of these scenarios are simulated using a computable general equilibrium (CGE) model of the Indian economy. The model has 17 commodity sectors and uses an econometrically estimated supply model for agriculture, which is disaggregated into rice, wheat, coarse cereals and other crops. Its key features are: a) trade quotas are imposed in some sectors, b) wages adjust partially to food prices in the medium run and are determined by market-clearing in the long run, and, c) it incorporates an econometrically estimated system of equations describing rice and wheat procurement. The base year for the model is 1983-84.

The trade liberalisation scenarios confirm that industrial protection is responsible for most of the taxation of agriculture and that while the effects of restrictions on agricultural trade may be large for some commodities, their overall effect on agriculture is small. In addition, since processed agricultural commodities are highly protected compared to the unprocessed commodities, extending trade liberalisation to the former has a large adverse impact on agriculture. The resulting decrease in agricultural prices fuels non-agricultural expansion and the combined effect of these is an increase in real incomes for all groups. However, in the long run these gains are smaller and become negligible for large farmers. When industrial protection is also removed, a large devaluation is needed to keep the balance of payments constant. GDP falls in the medium and long run. The accompanying removal of constraints on agricultural trade results in increased price transmission elasticities for all unprocessed agricultural commodities except coarse cereals, trade in which is negligible. As a result, rice and wheat prices increase substantially. But for other crops removal of protection and devaluation tend to counterbalance each other and the price changes little. As expected, urban incomes fall, agricultural income increases substantially and all rural classes' nominal incomes go up. However, these gains are undone by the increase in food prices for all but the medium and large farmers. While liberalisation has the desired effect of improving farm incentives it does little for the urban and rural poor. This points to a major policy dilemma. The growth-enhancing efficiency gains expected from liberalisation are operative only in the long run. Thus measures are required to protect the poor while these gains take effect.

Higher world agricultural prices have little effect if India's agricultural trade is not liberalised because trade shares in agriculture are small. Since India is a net exporter of agricultural commodities, India stands to gain from higher world prices and GDP increases in the long run when India also liberalises agricultural trade. However, the increase in domestic food prices skews the distribution of gains in favour of large and medium farmers and real incomes of the landless and small farmers fall. When higher world agricultural prices coincide with removal of protection to all sectors, the long-run decrease in GDP seen after complete liberalisation is reversed, but the gains are restricted to medium and large farmers and the distributional changes seen are larger. Thus higher world agricultural prices in the context of complete liberalisation intensify the policy dilemma referred to earlier.

The technical change scenarios demonstrate the key role of price flexibility in determining the distribution of gains from exogenous technical change. The observed low output elasticity of labour demand in agriculture suggests that rural net buyers of food may lose more from higher food prices than they gain from the increased employment resulting from supply response. In addition, these households derive a large fraction of total income from non-agricultural sources and an improvement in the terms of trade for agriculture will result in lower non-agricultural incomes. Thus if trade is held constant and yields increase, agricultural prices fall substantially. Non-agricultural classes' incomes go up as expected. Large farmers' real incomes fall, while other rural groups' real incomes increase. These losses can weaken producer incentives to save and invest, which will in turn result in slower productivity growth. If net exports are allowed to increase, the price decrease is moderated and the distribution of gains moves in favour of the farm sector and within the farm sector in favour of large farmers. Trade policy can therefore be used to maintain producer incentives and affect the distribution of gains from yield improvements. Government procurement can also be used for this purpose. The simulations demonstrate, however, that exporting rice to maintain producer incentives is preferable to procuring rice and selling it at a subsidised price on the domestic market.

The fertilizer subsidy scenario confirms in a general equilibrium system what has long been argued in a partial equilibrium framework, i.e. that the bulk of the subsidy accrues not to the agricultural sector but to the fertilizer sector. A novel finding emerges from the food subsidy scenarios. An increase in procurement and subsidised sales, if financed by an increase in indirect taxes, results in lower real incomes for all households, including the recipients of the increase in subsidised sales. However, if the increase is financed by an increase in direct taxation of large farmers and urban capitalists, it results in substantial benefits for the recipient household groups. Thus the distortionary costs of increased indirect taxation are larger at the margin than the marginal increase in income for the groups receiving the subsidy.

A common theme in these results is the importance of general equilibrium effects acting on the agricultural sector and the role of trade policy in affecting the terms of trade between agriculture and non-agriculture. Elucidating the impact of agricultural policy reform requires understanding of these crucial linkages. As this study demonstrates, a computable general equilibrium model provides an effective framework within which to examine these linkages using different scenarios of policy reforms.

Introduction

The significance of liberalisation of agricultural trade by the OECD countries under GATT for developing countries has been emphasized in several recent studies (Maunder and Valdés, Goldin and Knudsen). These studies suggest that liberalisation will result in higher world prices for agricultural commodities. Among the issues raised by agricultural trade liberalisation are the implications of higher agricultural prices for growth, welfare and distribution in developing countries and the question of how different developing countries ought to respond to these changes.

These issues are of particular relevance to India for several reasons. Firstly, agriculture remains a major sector of the Indian economy, accounting for 29.6 per cent of GDP and 61.5 per cent of employment[1]. Policies affecting agriculture will therefore have economy-wide repercussions. Secondly, the implications of policies affecting distribution and growth in agriculture are of immense importance for the great bulk of the poor, for whom agriculture provides livelihood, and also for the urban poor, whose real incomes are sensitive to food price changes. Lastly, the question of optimal response to world trade liberalisation is currently of much interest because the recent balance-of-payments crisis in India has forced the new government to question the wisdom of insulating the economy from the world market, as has been the policy so far, and has placed economic liberalisation squarely on the agenda for policy. Agricultural trade liberalisation and reductions in subsidies to agriculture are part of the reforms package sought to be implemented. Within the ranks of Indian economists there has long been a debate about the effectiveness and implications for distribution and growth of price and non-price interventions and incentives in agriculture[2]. How India ought to respond to higher world prices for agricultural products is an issue that will be eagerly seized upon in this debate.

This study uses a computable general equilibrium (CGE) model to address several key issues in the debate on agricultural policy reform. First, while trade liberalisation is expected to enhance efficiency, because resources are not perfectly mobile, it may fail to raise output in the short or medium run and result in lower welfare for some social groups, even in the long run. Who gains and who loses is likely to be a major concern of policy-makers, who recognise that higher food prices can have a large impact on the welfare of the poor. Secondly, since the industrial sector enjoys a far higher level of protection than does agriculture, the agricultural sector will be more sensitive to even small decreases in industrial protection than to complete liberalisation of agricultural trade. Thirdly, by raising trade shares, trade liberalisation will increase the exposure of the Indian economy to world price shocks, such as the increase in world agricultural prices resulting from agricultural trade liberalisation by the OECD countries, raising the possibility of large changes in terms of trade, welfare and distribution. Lastly, other agricultural policy reforms, such as reductions in fertilizer subsidy or changes in the food subsidy system, are also of concern because of their implications for public expenditure and distribution.

This study is divided into four chapters. The first chapter provides an overview of India's recent agricultural performance, the role of price and non-price factors and state intervention in agriculture, and of current issues of agricultural policy. The second chapter describes the model and the social accounting matrix around which it is built. The third chapter discusses the policy scenarios and simulation results. The last chapter summarises the results and conclusions for policy.

Notes and References

1. The share of GDP is for 1986, that of employment is for 1981. In addition, the share in GDP of industries based on agricultural inputs, such as food processing and cotton textiles, is 4 per cent.
2. See, for example, the articles by A.S. Kahlon and K. Subbarao in Dantwala (1986).

Chapter 1

A Review of Indian Agricultural Performance

1. Agricultural Growth

The performance of Indian agriculture in the half-century before independence in 1947 was dismal. As Blyn's painstaking study of the period from 1891 to 1947 shows, the annual rate of growth of production for food grains (cereals and pulses) was 0.11 per cent and for commercial crops 1.31 per cent. Total per capita output declined 0.72 per cent a year after 1911. With the partition of the subcontinent in 1947, about 32 per cent of the irrigated land in undivided India went to Pakistan (Dantwala, 1986). Severe food shortages led to cereal imports averaging 2.8 millions tons a year (or about 5 per cent of output) during the 1950s. Faced with chronic food deficits, the government invited a Ford Foundation team to study the problem. One of the team's recommendations was to concentrate efforts on crops and areas which had the best potential for increased production. This strategy led to the development of the Intensive Agricultural District Program (IADP), under which efforts to improve agricultural practices and to provide adequate inputs were restricted to areas of high growth potential. Only about 5 per cent of cultivable area was covered by IADP by 1967-68. Despite these efforts and some gains in production, the droughts of 1965-66 and 1966-67 resulted in massive decreases in output and large imports of wheat (10.4 million tons in 1966, or over 16 per cent of cereal output in 1965-66).

As Dantwala (1986) remarks, it was "sheer coincidence" that at about this time high-yielding varieties of rice and wheat became available and were introduced to India. Annual production in the five years after the drought years was over 20 per cent higher than annual production in the five years before 1965. But cereal imports remained significant, averaging 4.2 million tons between 1968 and 1976, then ceasing entirely in 1978 and 1979, and averaging 1.6 million tons between 1980 and 1985.

However, a statistical examination of growth rates (Table 1) shows that despite the much-vaunted Green Revolution, output growth rates for all crops except wheat and oilseeds were higher in the period 1950-65, before the Green Revolution, than in the period after the Green Revolution up to 1988[1]. Only in the case of wheat and oilseeds has there been an acceleration in growth, from 3.6 per cent to 5 per cent for wheat and 2.7 per cent to 3 per cent for oilseeds. The growth rate for rice fell marginally, from 3.1 per cent to 2.6 per cent. For crops which have by and large not benefitted from the new technology, such as coarse cereals and pulses, the fall in growth rates has been steeper, from 2 per cent to 0.6 per cent for coarse cereals and 1.1 per cent to 0.7 per cent for pulses. However, there was a fundamental difference in the nature of growth before and after the Green Revolution. Before the Green Revolution, total cropped area expanded at 1.6 per cent a year and yield increased at 1.3 per cent (Table 2), after the Green Revolution, these figures were 0.5 per cent and 1.9 per cent, respectively. Growth after the Green Revolution has therefore been based largely on yield increases, as expansion of the arable has slowed down.

Another characteristic of post-Green-Revolution agricultural growth, Rao *et al.* (1988) point out, is higher instability in yields and output for all major crops except wheat. Behind this rise in instability, they suggest, are the increased use of high-yielding varieties, which are more sensitive to timing and quantity of rainfall and irrigation, and the increased share in output of Western India, a region of poor and unstable rainfall.

2. Regional Differences

Large regional differences exist across India in agroclimatic potential, rural infrastructure, cropping patterns and yields, growth rates, input use, extent of irrigation, fertilizer use and adoption of high-yielding varieties. These in turn give rise to large differences in marketed surplus, agricultural incomes and extent of poverty. These differences are also reflected in differences in the responsiveness of agricultural supply and input use to price and non-price factors (Binswanger and Quizon, 1986). The findings from several recent studies are reviewed here.

Significant differences across agroclimatic regions in the nature and rate of growth of food grains production have been found by Rao *et al.* (1988) and Sarma and Gandhi (1990). Sarma and Gandhi divide the country into six regions. As Tables 3 and 4 demonstrate, there are wide divergences across regions in cropping patterns, population and output shares, fertilizer use and adoption of high-yielding varieties (HYVs) of cereals. Table 4 also shows how these patterns have changed over time, from 1980 to 1988. The Northern region includes the states of Punjab and Haryana, where the Green Revolution had its earliest and greatest impact, and other Northern states, excluding the state of Uttar Pradesh (which is a region by itself because of its size). The Northern region's shares of population (in 1980) and food grain output (in 1988/89) were 6.8 per cent and 17.1 per cent, respectively[2]. The major crops are wheat and rice, with shares of 64 per cent and 24 per cent. The Northern region is notable for its highly input-intensive agriculture based on extensive irrigation (74 per cent of cropped area was irrigated in 1986), widespread use of HYVs, a level of fertilizer use 82 per cent above the national average and food grain yields almost twice the national average. Accounting for 16.2 per cent of population and 21 per cent of food grain output, Uttar Pradesh is next to the Northern region in extent of irrigation, fertilizer use and HYV adoption.

The Central region covers the states of Rajasthan and Madhya Pradesh, regions of poorer infrastructure and greater aridity. Coarse grains and pulses are more important here. Food grain yields are lowest in this region, about 65 per cent of the national average. In this region adoption of HYVs doubled between 1980 and 1989

20

and fertilizer use almost tripled between 1980 and 1986. The Western region includes the well-watered coastal districts and the semi-arid interior of the Western states. Coarse cereals and pulses account for 62 per cent and rice for 26 per cent of output.

The Eastern region is predominantly a rice-growing area and has 26 per cent of the population and produces 20.1 per cent of food grain output. The Southern region is also a rice-growing area and produces no wheat. The irrigated coastal districts of this region are also areas where the new technology has had its highest impact. Though the extent of irrigation is lower than in the Northern states, fertilizer use is the highest in this region and the extent of HYV adoption is also high.

Sarma and Gandhi analyse growth of production, cropped area and yield for rice, wheat, coarse cereals, all cereals, pulses and food grains for these six regions over the period before the Green Revolution (Period 1, from 1952/53-1964/65) and the period thereafter (which they divide into two sub-periods, Period 2, from 1967/68-1975/76 and Period 3, from 1975/76 to 1983/84; in this study Period 3 has been extended to 1988/90). Growth rates for production and yield of total food grains increased in the Northern region and Uttar Pradesh (for which the output and yield growth rates accelerated to 4.6 per cent and 4.1 per cent in the last period from less than 1 per cent in the previous periods, increases of great significance given this region's share of output and population). In the Eastern and Central regions, the growth rate for total food grains dipped in Period 2 before returning in Period 3 to a value close to that in Period 1[3]. Yields increased steadily in the Southern region and at an increasing rate in the Central region. In the Western region, output and yield increased at about the same rate in Periods 1 and 2, but fell in Period 3. Since fertilizer use and adoption of HYVs continued to increase in this region, Sarma and Gandhi surmise that the stagnation in the last period was the result of poor rainfall. Output growth in the Southern region was lower in Period 3 because of a marked shift away from food grains. A less pronounced shift away from food grains was also observed in this period in the Western, Central and Eastern regions. Thus area under food grains continued to increase in the second half of the post-Green Revolution period only in the Northern region and Uttar Pradesh.

The cropwise growth rates reveal interesting contrasts. In the case of rice, the growth rate of yields rose sharply in Period 2 in the Northern region and fell equally sharply in Period 3; however, the shift towards rice accelerated in Period 3. In Uttar Pradesh and the Southern region, rice yields increased at an accelerating rate. In the Eastern and Central regions, rice yields declined after the Green Revolution, during Period 2, and grew fastest in Period 3, possibly because of greater initial difficulty with the new technology. In the Western region the production of all cereals stagnated or fell during Period 3. In the case of wheat, only in the Northern region and Uttar Pradesh did area expansion continue in Period 3. In the other regions (excluding the Southern region, where wheat production is small) area under wheat either ceased to expand or decreased in Period 3. But in the Central region wheat output continued to increase rapidly as yields increased. In the Eastern region, a large shift to wheat and high yield growth in Period 2 was followed by no further area expansion and substantially lower yield growth. By Period 3, there was a movement away from cereals towards pulses in the Eastern, Western and Southern regions, areas of low but increasing yields, while pulses gave way to cereals in the other regions, including the regions with the highest pulse yields, Uttar Pradesh and the Northern region. There were also substantial shifts away from coarse cereals in all regions after the Green

Revolution. Rapid adoption of HYV sorghum in the Western region resulted in higher yield growth for coarse cereals, the major crop in this region, in Period 2, but yield growth became negative in Period 3, during which all cereals were adversely affected. Coarse cereals are also the major crop in the Central region, but here yield growth rates remained below 1 per cent in all periods.

Differences in output growth rates for wheat and rice are responsible for much of the differences across regions in growth rates of food grain production. This is strikingly demonstrated in the case of rice, where the share of the three Northern states of Punjab, Haryana and Uttar Pradesh in total rice production more than doubled from 10.4 per cent during 1963-65 to 22.5 per cent over the period 1983-85 and the share of three major Eastern states (West Bengal, Orissa and Bihar) fell from 38.1 per cent to 28.2 per cent (Rao et al., 1988; Table 4.5).

Another important manifestation of growing regional differences is in the ratios of marketed surplus to output, which are shown in Table 6 for the period 1979/80-1982/83 for major producing states. Given that growth rates of rice and wheat production are highest for Punjab, Haryana and Uttar Pradesh, the high ratio of marketed surplus to output for these states (reaching over 90 per cent for rice in Punjab and Haryana) implies that the share of these states in the marketed surplus of rice and wheat has been increasing rapidly over time. The concentration of marketed surplus in these states has implications for price policy, trade and food security policies, as will be seen below.

In addition to the differences across regions in input use seen in Table 4, substantial differences also exist across regions in the use of machinery, draft animal power and human labour. These differences in input use and in yields are reflected in wide variations in production costs and factor shares for the same crop across regions. These variations are shown for rice and wheat in Table 7. Variations in labour use for a wide variety of crops are to be seen in Table 8. One consequence of these variations is that uniform pricing policies can have widely differing impacts across regions on profitability and on income distribution.

3. Government Intervention and Producer Incentives[4]

Price Policy

Governments the world over intervene in agricultural markets and the Indian government is no exception. The government intervenes extensively in product markets and in domestic and external trade, it maintains buffer stocks and it provides rations of food commodities at subsidised prices to consumers. The government also intervenes in input markets. This intervention takes several forms. Inputs, such as fertilizer, seeds, electricity and water, are produced and distributed by public sector agencies and government-owned banks provide subsidised credit to agriculture. The government also controls imports, pricing and distribution of fertilizers.

Government intervention in the food-grain market began during the Second World War, when it became necessary to procure cereal supplies and to ration food in urban areas. In the post-war period domestic procurement was low until the 1960s and public distribution of cereals was met largely through imports. With the introduction of high-yielding varieties and the associated cultivation practices in the early 1960s, it was thought necessary to provide support prices to encourage adoption of the new technology. The Agricultural Prices Commission (APC) was set up for this purpose and was charged with setting support prices that covered the average cost of production, including costs of fixed capital, rental of owned land and the imputed cost of family labour[5]. In addition, the government announces procurement prices, i.e. prices at which the government would buy the quantities that it desired. The procurement system in the past was bolstered by restrictions on transport of cereals, which had the effect of lowering prices in surplus regions, thereby enabling the government to obtain cereals at lower prices[6]. With the accumulation of large inventories of cereals by the government since the late 1970s, these restrictions have been removed and procurement prices have gradually taken on the role of support prices, i.e. the government stands ready to purchase whatever it is offered at the procurement price[7]. Rice procurement, however, is still accomplished through a levy, but Gulati and Sharma (1990b) suggest that the effectiveness of the levy depends on the relative attractiveness of sales to the government compared to open market sales. In recent years, the ratio of procurement to total output has ranged from 16 per cent to 20 per cent for wheat and 10 per cent to 15 per cent for rice.

Subbarao (1991) reviews the effect of these incentives on producers of rice and wheat, the major crops. Until the mid-1960s the procurement price for wheat was less than the average cost of production in most states, but the farm harvest price was above the procurement price and above average costs, while the volume of procurement was minimal. As a result, government intervention did not damage producer incentives during this period[8]. After 1967-68, the procurement price was higher than average cost in every state. In the case of rice, the procurement price was higher than the cost of production in the states of Punjab, Bihar, Madhya Pradesh and Orissa and lower than the cost of production in some years in the states of West Bengal and Andhra Pradesh. Unlike wheat, the rice procurement price may have been unfavourable in some years for some states[9]. For the post-Green Revolution period, Subbarao (1991) concludes that government intervention maintained producer incentives by ensuring that prices remained above average costs, thus encouraging productivity growth for the two major crops[10]. Furthermore, as incremental increases in rice and wheat output and marketed surplus have been concentrated in the Northern states of Punjab, Haryana and Uttar Pradesh, in this surplus region market prices for rice and wheat have tended to fall and converge towards procurement prices, so that procurement no longer represents a tax[11]. As a result of the increase in this region's share of output and marketed surplus and because of economies of scale in procurement activities, procurement is heavily concentrated here. From 1986-87 to 1988-89, for example, these states' share in wheat procurement was 99.27 per cent and in rice procurement 63.31 per cent (Gulati and Sharma, 1991; Tables 1 and 2). In the other states, where the marketed surplus is smaller, market prices have remained above average costs and in most cases above procurement prices and the share of these states in government purchases has remained small. The procurement operations therefore mostly benefit rice and wheat growers in high-productivity regions. Surplus producers in other regions have not been losers because market prices in these regions have been high enough to ensure an adequate return to the producer (Table 9).

Price support operations and other interventions for other crops have in general not been as extensive (Gulati and Sharma, 1991). For example, market prices for coarse cereals have often fallen below the support price without the government entering the market and the quantity procured has always been small. In the case of pulses, the support prices have in recent years always been well below market prices. This has often been the case also for oilseeds. A public sector agency also maintains buffer stocks of edible oils in order to support groundnut prices and to stabilize groundnut oil prices.

Cotton and sugar cane are the other major crops subject to intervention. Cotton price support and stabilization is undertaken by two agencies, one nationwide and the other restricted to the major cotton-producing state of Maharashtra, which often act at cross purposes, with the Maharashtra agency offering a higher price than the national agency and thereby attracting cotton imports from other states. Sugar and sugar cane are also subject to price supports and controls. Sugar cane prices are largely determined by the individual state governments and vary substantially from state to state. Large-scale sugar producers have to sell part of their production to the government at below market price (which channels this sugar to the public distribution system or sells it on the open market to control prices) and are free to sell the rest on the open market. The price the government pays is based on production costs and other criteria. The net effect has been to subsidise mills operating in north India, where sugar content of cane is low, and tax mills in Western and Southern India, which have lower costs of production because of the higher sugar content of cane. The fraction of levy has varied from zero in some years to 100 per cent in other years. A large part of sugar cane output escapes government controls because it is used by small-scale producers for producing various forms of unrefined sugar.

Input Subsidies

The major subsidies on agricultural inputs are on fertilizers, irrigation, electricity and credit. While the original rationale for providing input subsidies was that of encouraging adoption of modern inputs and that input subsidies were an inexpensive way to stimulate agricultural supply without raising output prices, these subsidies have shot up in recent years. The fertilizer subsidy rose from around Rs 4 billion ($500 million) in the early 1980s to Rs 46 billion ($2.7 billion) in 1989-90. Gulati and Sharma (1991) estimate that the subsidy on electricity rose from Rs 3.6 billion ($450 million) in 1980-81 to Rs 34.7 billion ($2 billion) in 1989-90 (about Rs 20 billion at 1980 prices). The subsidy rate for electricity was a staggering 82 per cent in 1989-90[12]. Gulati and Sharma (1991) also estimate the implicit subsidy on irrigation and on credit. They find the average annual irrigation subsidy from 1974 to 1989 to have been Rs 100 billion ($5.9 billion) at 1989 prices and the average credit subsidy to have been Rs 12 billion ($700 million) a year[13].

4. The Public Distribution System

As seen in the previous section, public distribution began as an effort to provision the cities during a time of chronic scarcity of food. It was later extended to rural areas of high scarcity, such as the state of Kerala (which has a chronic food deficit because it specialises in plantation crops). Subbarao (1991) argues that during this time the system was essentially a "supply-equalising intervention" and that after the Green Revolution it evolved into a programme to provide subsidised food to poor households, i.e. into a "poverty-alleviation intervention".

However, the system does not necessarily benefit the poor. For one thing, in most states there is no attempt to limit access to subsidised food to the poor[14]. Moreover, states with large numbers of poor people — the Northern and Central states of Uttar Pradesh, Bihar, Madhya Pradesh and Rajasthan — have a small share of total subsidised sales. In addition, coverage of rural areas, where the bulk of the poor are located, is minimal except in the states of Kerala, Andhra Pradesh, Tamil Nadu and Gujarat. But some of these states have found it difficult to provide subsidised food to the entire eligible population for budgetary reasons. George (1988) suggests that even in these states, distribution of rations is targeted toward the poor only in Kerala, while in Tamil Nadu it is biased toward the better off and in Gujarat rations are uniformly distributed. In Kerala the system appears to be well-targeted and budgetary pressures have been eased by charging the rich higher prices than the poor.

The nutritional benefits of subsidised rations appear to be substantial in Gujarat and Kerala, where the subsidy increases calorie intake for the lowest expenditure group by over 10 per cent in Gujarat and 17 per cent in Kerala (George 1988)[15]. The evidence suggests that well-targeted public distribution programmes that cover rural and urban areas can protect the poor in times of scarcity and improve their nutrition. Subbarao (1991) argues that despite the success of these programmes in some states, "there has been a pervasive resistance to establish[ing] a stable, long-run targeted distribution for the poor in the States which have a substantial proportion of the nation's population below the poverty line." (p. 16)

The budgetary cost of running the public distribution and procurement system has increased substantially over time (Table 10). The budgetary cost has two components, the so-called consumer subsidy and the carrying cost of the buffer stock. The consumer subsidy per unit is the difference between procurement price plus costs of procurement and distribution and the issue (or sale) price. Two factors are responsible for the increase in subsidy. Firstly, as Gulati and Sharma (1991) note, the costs of procurement and distribution (i.e. marketing margins) have been going up faster than the wholesale price index and faster than procurement prices. Secondly, carrying charges have gone up as the level of stocks increased substantially during the early 1980s.

The true consumer subsidy is clearly the difference between the price the consumer pays for subsidised food and the retail price. But what part of the subsidy is a subsidy to consumers is unclear for two reasons. Firstly, the "issue" price quoted by the government and recorded in the data is merely the price the central government charges the state governments for subsidised foods. The price the consumer pays is higher by an unknown amount. Secondly, given the differences in quality involved it is not clear what retail price should be used for the price comparison. Thirdly, allowance has to be made for "leakages" of subsidised food commodities to the open market.

5. Intervention in External Trade

Gulati and Sharma (1991) review government intervention in external trade in agricultural products. In general, exports of commodities in short supply in India are prohibited and imports of such commodities is permitted. Thus exports of natural rubber, pulses and oilseeds are banned (except groundnuts for direct consumption). Imports of pulses are subject to only a 10 per cent duty. Import of edible oils is a government monopoly, as are imports and exports of sugar. Imports of rice and wheat are also effectively a government monopoly. Exports are subject to quotas and in the case of the superfine *basmati* grade of rice, to a minimum export price. Cotton imports are the domain of a state agency and cotton exports are subject to quotas and a minimum export price.

The effects of these policies would be to make domestic prices and world prices differ. Gulati and Sharma (1991) provide estimates of nominal and effective protection coefficients (NPCs and EPCs) for several crops and states, considering each crop as an exportable and as an importable. On the importable hypothesis the average NPC for wheat from 1980-81 to 1986-87 is 0.80, while that for rice is 0.67. On the exportable hypothesis, these become 1.34 and 0.87, respectively. The other major taxed crop they study is cotton. The oilseeds are by and large highly protected with NPCs around 1.5 on the importable hypothesis. Lastly, sugar cane is also highly protected, with average NPCs of 1.55 and 2.10 on the importable and exportable hypotheses. Differences in input use and transport costs result in substantial variation across states in NPCs and EPCs. Thus, on the importable hypothesis the NPC in 1986 for wheat ranged from 0.75 in Madhya Pradesh to 0.99 in Punjab, while that for rice ranged from 0.76 in Orissa to 0.90 in Punjab. These variations are greatest for cotton and sugar cane, prices for which are set at widely differing levels from state to state. Similar differences can be observed for EPCs. The range of EPCs and NPCs observed leads Subbarao (1991) to conclude that the net effect of agricultural trade policies on agriculture in recent years may have been neutral or only slightly taxed.

Gulati and Sharma (1991) also adjust for subsidies on non-traded inputs to arrive at effective subsidy coefficients (ESCs) for these crops. These estimates suggest that except for cotton all the crops studied are either highly protected or only slightly taxed and that subsidies on non-traded inputs are an important component of effective incentives in agriculture. The sometimes large differences in ESCs/EPCs across states and the emerging regional concentration of marketed surplus suggests that, just as in the case of price policy, changes in world prices or in trade policies can have very different effects on different regions.

Notes and References

1. This is the case even if the drought years 1966 and 1967 are dropped. Table 2 (Subbarao *et al.*, 1988) shows that for the period up to 1985 only in the case of wheat did output grow faster after the Green Revolution after adjusting for fluctuations in rainfall. It should be noted that even for oilseeds, the unadjusted growth rate up to 1985 was lower than the unadjusted growth rate in the period before 1965.

2. Population data are for 1981 since results from the 1991 census are not yet available.

3. Growth rates are highly unstable so these trends in growth rates must be interpreted carefully. For example, the growth rate for total food grains in the Eastern region was -0.22 per cent between 1975/76 and 1983/84 while the growth rate over 1975/76-1988/89 was 1.96 per cent.

4. This section draws heavily on Subbarao (1991) and Gulati and Sharma (1991).

5. The commission now announces support prices for 20 crops. In 1980, the terms of reference of the commission were changed, asking it to take into account factors other than the cost of cultivation, such as movements in the net barter terms of trade between agriculture and industry. The commission was also renamed as Commission on Agricultural Costs and Prices.

6. As Gulati and Sharma (1991) point out, a number of procurement measures have been used, including monopoly purchase, levy on producers or traders and millers, pre-emptive purchases, and so on.

7. Public stocks of food grains were over 20 million tons in 1984, 1985 and 1986 and declined to 12 million tons in 1989. Expressed as a proportion of production, stocks were 17 per cent, 19.8 per cent, 18 per cent and 8.1 per cent of output in these years.

8. Of course, producer prices would have been higher had the government not taken recourse to subsidised wheat imports from the United States in these years.

9. Gulati and Sharma (1990b) reach the same conclusion. De Janvry and Subbarao (1986) note that Mitra (1977) argues that the increase in rice procurement prices was no accident. Once the rich farmers of Punjab started growing rice as a summer crop, the government was forced to raise the procurement price.

10. Moreover, Hayami, Otsuka and Subbarao (1982) argue that procurement operations actually raise the average price received by the farmer over the level that would prevail in the absence of procurement.

11. Unfortunately, Table 9 (from Subbarao, 1991) provides farm harvest price for wheat in Punjab and Haryana for only a single year, so the data in this table cannot be used to buttress Subbarao's conclusion that harvest and market prices converged for wheat in these states.

12. In many states electricity is supplied at a flat rate to farmers based on the size of the farm machinery to be operated (usually an electric pump).

13. Water charges are usually based on a flat rate system and the rates are set according to the crop to be grown. Because of the lack of incentive to limit water use and the ease of evading or subverting administrative controls on water use, water distribution in irrigation schemes is often highly inequitable, with those at the head of the distributory appropriating whatever water they need to cultivate water-intensive crops and leaving little for tail-enders. The result, of course, is that the irrigation subsidy is inequitably distributed and gains from irrigation are not maximised. The irrigation subsidy estimates must be interpreted with caution because Gulati and Sharma use three methods of estimation which give widely different results.

14. However, the lower quality of items sold by ration shops results in some degree of automatic targeting.

15. The provision of subsidised food in the rural areas appears to have other benefits also. Subbarao (1991) reports that in Andhra Pradesh one effect of the provision of cheap rice in the countryside is that agricultural labourers no longer have to enter into long-term labour contracts with landlords in exchange for consumption loans. Another advantage became apparent during the drought of 1981, when several states set up food-for-work programmes to alleviate scarcity. States that had well-established rural public distribution systems were able to use them to support these food-for-work programmes.

Chapter 2

The Social Accounting Matrix and the Model

1. The Social Accounting Matrix

The social accounting matrix (SAM) developed for this study is shown in aggregated form in Table 11. This SAM is at producer prices. The SAM has 17 activities and 17 commodities and seven household classes. The activities and commodities are: rice, wheat, coarse cereals, other crops, dairy products, meat, edible oils, sugar, other processed foods, textiles, consumer goods, intermediates, durables, services, public administration, draught animal services and fertilizer. The level of disaggregation and the choice of accounts are influenced by the issues to be addressed in the CGE model and the availability of data. Thus the disaggregation of agriculture into four sectors (rice, wheat, coarse cereals and other crops) and of agricultural inputs into fertilizers and draught animal services is dictated by the importance of rice and wheat for policy and the availability of a supply system at this level of sectoral detail. The level of sectoral detail of available demand systems determines the choice of other commodity accounts.

Other accounts in the unaggregated SAM include the government, the capital account, changes in stocks, the rest of the world, direct taxes, import duties, import subsidies, export duties, export subsidies, irrigation subsidy, other subsidies, other indirect taxes and accounts for agricultural wages, agricultural profits, non-agricultural wages, non-agricultural profits and income of the self-employed in non-agriculture[1]. The household groups are defined in a manner similar to that in the SAM constructed by de Janvry and Subbarao (1986). Following them, I divide rural households into four classes: landless agricultural labourers, small farmers (0-0.85 ha), medium farmers (0.85-3.27 ha) and large farmers (above 3.27 ha)[2]. The rural landless employed in non-agricultural activities were considered part of the urban (strictly speaking, non-agricultural) classes. The urban households were divided into workers and the self-employed. The latter category was further divided into the lowest 82 per cent of the self-employed (the "marginals") and the upper 18 per cent (the "capitalists"). The urban households receive no agricultural income. However, the rural households receive income from non-agricultural wages, profits and self-employment. The construction of the SAM is discussed in the appendix.

The population in each class, their sources of income, per capita income and expenditure are shown in Table 12. As can be seen from this table, except for the large farmer households, all other rural classes get between a fourth and a third of their income from non-agricultural sources. The consumer subsidy on food makes only a small contribution to income (in constructing the SAM, I assumed that the subsidy went only to the urban classes of worker and marginal households on an equal per capita basis).

2. The Model

Several computable general equilibrium models for the Indian economy have been developed in recent years. Notable among these are those of Rattso (1990), Sarkar (1990), de Janvry and Subbarao (1986) and Narayana, Parikh and Srinivasan (1991) and the multimarket model of Binswanger and Quizon (1986). The work of Rattso and Sarkar focuses on macroeconomic issues, such as inflation and wage indexation, in the structuralist tradition made popular by Lance Taylor. More relevant here are the models of Binswanger and Quizon, de Janvry and Subbarao, and Narayana *et al.*, which focus on the agricultural sector.

In the Binswanger-Quizon model the non-agricultural sector is a residual and is exogenous. There are four agricultural commodities: rice, wheat, coarse cereals and other crops, and three inputs: labour, draft animal services and fertilizer. Supply and demand functions are obtained from a profit function estimated using a flexible functional form. Shifters in these equations include neutral technical change, rainfall, high-yielding varieties and farm capital. Households are divided into four rural and four urban quartiles. Foreign trade and government revenues and expenditure are not modelled explicitly[3]. The authors solve a linear approximation to the model. Among the issues examined by them are the implications of trade for the distribution of gains from technical change and the effects of a fertilizer subsidy.

The model of de Janvry and Subbarao is also in the structuralist tradition. Agriculture is taken to be a flexible-price sector with prices determined by market clearing. Pricing in industry and services is determined by a mark-up over cost and supply adjusts, the assumption being that these sectors are characterised by excess capacity. The focus is on the role of price and non-price interventions in agriculture and their effects on distribution. The policy instruments considered are price supports, increases in the minimum wage, procurement (i.e. government purchases) of crops for subsequent subsidised sale, investment in irrigation, and food subsidies. Government expenditures and revenue are explicitly modelled, so that the budgetary implications of these policy instruments can be examined. However, foreign trade is taken to be exogenous and is not modelled. Unlike the Binswanger-Quizon model, the de Janvry-Subbarao model is built around a social accounting matrix (SAM). As noted earlier, the SAM developed for this study is based in part on the de Janvry-Subbarao SAM.

The model of Narayana *et al.* has two special features. Firstly, there is no labour market in the model, the assumption being that households receive fixed shares of value added in each sector, hardly an innocuous assumption for an agrarian economy with a large number of landless households. Secondly, the model seeks to determine the volume and direction of agricultural trade endogenously under the assumption that exports, imports and domestic production are perfect substitutes, so that the direction of trade is determined by prices and transport margins.

The model presented here combines Binswanger-Quizon's multi-market approach to modelling agricultural supply and input demands with the traditional CGE production approach for the other sectors. The multi-market approach has several advantages. Unlike in the traditional CGE model, more factors than labour and capital can be accommodated. Hence the effects of fertilizer pricing policies on fertilizer use and output can be worked out. Furthermore, substitution between crops is explicitly modelled. Lastly, the multi-market supply and demand equations have the virtue of being econometrically estimated so that model calibration, one of the "grey" areas of CGE work, becomes a less onerous task[4].

A detailed description of the model is provided in the appendix. The discussion here will concentrate on features of the model that are specific to it, such as the agricultural supply model, the treatment of the incomes of the self-employed and the modelling of procurement and subsidised sales.

2.1 The Self-employed and the Informal Sector

Output and value added in the informal sector are assumed to be proportional to that in the formal sector and value added in the informal sector is assumed to flow in fixed proportions to non-agricultural wages, non-agricultural profits and the self-employed[5]. The production function and profit maximisation determine output and value added in the formal sector. The informal sector's output and value added are simply fixed multiples of output and value added in the formal sector.

There are several deficiencies in this model of the informal sector; for example, there is neither a separate informal labour market, nor a separate production function which would take into account the informal sector's lower capital intensity, nor a different set of consumption and production linkages between the informal sector and agriculture. The lack of data on the informal sector stands in the way of more realistic modelling.

2.2 The Agricultural Supply Model

The agricultural supply model is based on the normalised quadratic profit function. The supply and demand equations obtained from this specification take the following form:

$$X_i/\alpha_i = a_i + \sum_{j=1}^{n-1} b_{ij} \, \alpha_j \, P_j/P_n \tag{1a}$$

for the first $n\text{-}1$ outputs and inputs. For the last output or input:

$$X_n/\alpha_n = a_0 - \frac{1}{2} \sum_{ij=1}^{n-1} b_{ij} \, P_i \, P_j \, \alpha_i \, \alpha_j/P_n^2 \tag{1b}$$

31

Here the index i runs over inputs and outputs, the convention being that when i represents an input, the corresponding X_i has a negative sign. The P_i are the relevant prices (i.e. producer price exclusive of tax for an output, price inclusive of tax for a material input, the wage for agricultural labour) and the a_i and the b_{ij} are econometrically estimated parameters. The first m commodities are outputs and the last $n - m$ are inputs. The α_i are parameters for neutral technical change, i.e. the α_i are 1 for all inputs and differ from unity only for outputs. An increase in yields that is the result of neutral technical change would increase the corresponding α_i. Binswanger and Quizon provide estimates of elasticities obtained from such a specification[6]. These elasticities were assumed to hold in the base year. The parameters b_{ij} need to satisfy a symmetry constraint, $b_{ij} = b_{ji}$. The b_{ij} computed from the elasticities and the base year values of X_i and P_i may not satisfy this constraint. The elasticities were therefore modified using a least-squares criterion to satisfy this constraint. The original and modified elasticities are shown in Table 13. The system of supply and demand equations gives the supply of the four crops and demand for draft animal services, fertilizer and labour. Demands for other inputs are obtained using the input-output coefficients.

2.3 The Procurement and Public Distribution Model

Gulati and Sharma (1990b) have studied the relationship between quantity procured, quantity of output, the ratio of procurement price to wholesale market price and restrictions on internal trade. In the case of rice, they find that the size of the levy (in per cent) is an important determinant of procurement and that the price ratio is insignificant except in the state of Andhra Pradesh. However, when they estimate the procurement equation for the country as a whole, they drop the levy term and retain the price ratio, possibly because it is difficult to define the levy variable for the entire country. But the coefficient on the price variable is then insignificant. However, for want of anything better, I have chosen to use this equation. The wheat equation does not present this problem because no levy exists for wheat. At least for wheat, the case can be made that procurement is no longer a tax on the producer and that the reason the procurement price differs from the open market price is because of differences in quality between what is sold to the government and what is sold on the open market and because of differences in timing of sales.

The wheat and rice procurement equations are as follows:

$$p_x x_d = p_m q_m + p_{pr} q_{pr} \tag{2}$$

$$x_d = q_m + q_{pr} \tag{3}$$

$$q_{pr} = a_0 + a_1 x_d + a_2 p_{pr}/p_m \tag{4}$$

Here, equation 2 defines the price received by the farmer, p_x, as the average of the procurement price, p_{pr}, and the market price, p_m. Equation 3 states that total output, x_d, equals sales on the open market, q_m, plus procurement, q_{pr}. Equation 4 is the procurement equation, which states that the amount procured is a linear function of output and the ratio of procurement to open market price. The marginal procurement propensity a_1 is 0.12 in the case of rice and 0.25 in the case of wheat. When procurement is measured in millions of tons, the coefficient of the price ratio is 3.29 for rice and 5.18 for wheat. In the base year the price ratios were 0.6961 for rice and

0.9042 for wheat (Gulati and Sharma, 1990b) and the elasticity of procurement with respect to output is 1.37 for wheat and 1.0 for rice, and with respect to the price ratio, 0.57 for wheat and 0.32 for rice. One difficulty with this functional form is its linearity. One would expect different behaviour when the procurement price is close to the open market price than when it is well below the open market price. Another difficulty is that this formulation does not restrict the procurement price to lie below the open market price. These problems are less important for rice, for which the price ratio is well below 1.

The government buys an amount q_{pr} at a price p_{pr}, incurs costs of procurement and distribution and of storage and sells a quantity q_s at a price p_s. The costs to the government are given by the following equations.

$$C_{st} = \sum_{i \in R} (S_{0i} + \tfrac{1}{2}(q_{pri} - q_{si})) C_i, \quad R = (\text{rice,wheat})$$

$$C_{pr} = \sum_{i \in R} (p_{pri} + \bar{p}\, m_{pri} - p_{si})\, q_{si}$$

Here S_{0i} is the initial stock of commodity i, C_i the unit cost of storage and C_{st} is the cost of storage, which is proportional to the average of stocks at the beginning and end of the year. C_{pr} is the subsidy on sales and is given by the difference between the sum of procurement prices (p_{pri}) and procurement and distribution margins (m_{pri}) multiplied by the price index $(\bar{p})$ and the sale price (p_{si}) times the quantity sold.

I assume that subsidised sales are inframarginal, so that the subsidy can be treated as a transfer. Note that this means that when computing the value of absorption, the amount sold, q_s, must be valued at the procurement price, p_{pr}, and not the sale price, p_s. The consumer subsidy is then the difference between retail price and subsidised sale price times the quantity sold. The difficulty with this is that the retail price in the model is nowhere near the true retail price, i.e. it is not high enough. The reason for this is that the retail price differs from the wholesale price by the trade and transport margins. Since the share of home consumption is high, the calculated trade and transport margins are too low because they are obtained by dividing the trade and transport services associated with absorption by the total output and not by only that part of output which has gone through the market. To circumvent this problem, I use a higher mark-up in defining the consumer subsidy, so that the retail price used for this purpose is more realistic.

$$C_{con} = \sum_{i \in R} ((1 + r_i) p_i - p_{si})\, q_{si}$$

Here, p_i is the producer price inclusive of taxes, r_i is the higher mark-up used and C_{con} is the subsidy to consumers. The difference between the cost to government, C_{pr}, and the consumer subsidy, C_{con}, is treated as purchase of trade and transport services by the government, as is the storage cost, C_{st}. The total subsidy paid by the government (excluding storage costs for food stocks) in the base year was Rs 9.3 billion and the transfer to households was Rs 6.0 billion[7].

2.4 The Demand Model

The model of demand is the familiar LES (linear expenditure system). The parameters are based on estimates by Radhakrishna and Murty (1980). They estimated LES models for five urban and five rural household groups for thirteen commodities. These commodities are: rice, wheat, coarse cereals, dairy products, edible oils, meat, sugar, pulses, fruits and vegetables, other food, clothing, fuel and light, and other non-foods. Pulses and fruits and vegetables are aggregated to match the category other crops in the agricultural supply system. Other food is matched with other processed foods (excluding sugar and edible oils) from the input-output table. In addition, fuel and light and other non-food are aggregated giving eleven commodities in all. The estimated expenditure elasticities for these commodities were plotted against the mean expenditure for the five urban and five rural groups. From these graphs predicted values of the expenditure elasticities were read off at the mean (deflated) expenditure levels for the seven household groups in the SAM. A similar exercise with the Frisch parameter gave estimates of the Frisch parameter for each household group. Combining the estimated Frisch parameters and expenditure elasticities with the base-year budget shares and prices, the entire set of LES parameters was obtained for each household group [cf. Dervis *et al.* (1982), Appendix A.5].

To disaggregate the other non-foods category further, I assume that utilities are separable and that the utility function for other non-foods is a Cobb-Douglas function, the arguments being the quantities of consumer goods, intermediates, durables and services consumed. The price of other non-foods is then the geometric mean of the prices of these commodities, the weights being their budget shares, which are constant and remain at their base-year levels[8]. It is easy to obtain the indirect utility and expenditure functions from this demand system. The expenditure function, in particular, is used to compute compensating variations to obtain group-specific price indices and real incomes.

2.5 External Trade

As is common in the CGE modelling literature, imperfect substitutability of imports and domestic production and of exports and domestic sales is assumed. Absorption is written as a CES aggregation of domestic sales and imports, the assumption being that cost minimisation determines the ratio of imports to consumption of the domestic product. Similarly, total output is a CET function of domestic sales and exports and revenue maximisation determines the ratio of exports to domestic sales. The elasticities specified are shown in Table 14. They are high for rice, wheat, sugar, fertilizer and edible oils and lower for aggregates such as other crops and manufactured products. The elasticities are also higher for imports than for exports, reflecting the notion that it is always easier to change the level of imports than that of exports.

The prevalence of restrictions on external trade means recorded tariff rates (computed from data accompanying the input-output table) differ from nominal rates of protection based on observed differences between domestic and world prices as Table 14 shows. The nominal protection coefficients for agriculture are obtained from Gulati and Sharma (1991). NPCs for many of the crops in the other crops group are not known, so the value used for this group should not be treated as authoritative. For industry, NPCs are reported in a recent World Bank country study (1989). However, this study does not provide precise numerical estimates, only three ranges, below 30 per cent, between 30 per cent and 70 per cent and above 70 per cent. These were replaced by 15 per cent, 50 per cent and 100 per cent and production-weighted averages taken to obtain NPCs at the desired level of aggregation (reported in Table 14). In the case of agricultural commodities, restrictions on imports and exports exist, which is not the case with industrial commodities, for which only imports are restricted. By comparing NPCs and recorded tariff rates some idea may be had of the importance of non-price barriers. Thus rice is taxed under both importable and exportable hypotheses, which suggests that exports are restricted. Wheat is taxed as an importable and protected as an exportable, so trade restrictions cannot be binding. Coarse cereals are essentially non-tradables. For other crops, the NPC (assumed to be 1.4) exceeds the import tariff plus 1, implying that imports are restricted. No estimate of NPC is available for dairy products and meat, fish and eggs. For all the industrial products, the estimated NPC exceeds the import tariff rate, so that imports are restricted.

As these studies have shown, domestic prices diverge from border prices for many tradables. However, it is not clear what part of this divergence is accounted for by restrictions on trade and what part by imperfect substitutability between a commodity sold on the home market and the same commodity traded on the world market. It would be incorrect to ascribe the observed price wedges entirely to the existence of trade restrictions; to do so would overestimate the degree to which trade is restricted. Restrictions on imports are modelled as "fix-price" rationing (Dervis *et al.*, p. 293)[9].

$$X = a \left(\theta M^\rho + (1 - \theta) D^\rho \right)^{1/\rho} \tag{5}$$

$$(M/D)^* = \left(\frac{(1 - \theta) P_M}{\theta P_D} \right)^{1/(\rho - 1)}; \quad M/D = k(M/D)^* \tag{6}$$

As in the standard Armington specification, domestic absorption, X, is a CES aggregate of domestic sales, D, and imports, M, and the cost-minimising or desired ratio of imports to domestic sales, $(M/D)^*$, is given by equation 6, where P_M and P_D are the price of imports and domestic sales, respectively. However, because of restrictions on imports, the actual ratio of imports to domestic sales, (M/D) is a fraction k of the desired ratio, $(M/D)^{*}$[10]. Implicit in this formulation is the assumption that users pay the border price, i.e., no premium income is generated. This assumption is valid if scarce imports are allocated administratively and resale is prohibited, which is more likely to be the case for producer goods than for consumer goods. In the case of India, imports of consumer goods are small so this treatment of rationing, while it may be unrealistic for consumer goods sectors, is not too inaccurate overall.

However, no estimates are available for the degree to which imports and exports are rationed. In the absence of such estimates, I proceed as follows. The degree of import (or export) rationing, the parameter k, is chosen such that removing rationing (i.e. setting k equal to unity) results in what are judged to be reasonable changes in domestic prices and trade ratios. The rationing factor used and the price and trade changes observed are shown below.

Commodity	Actual Tariff	Rationing Factor	Domestic Prices[a]		Export or Import Ratio (%)	
			with	without	with	without
			rationing		rationing	
Rice	—	0.2	0.890	0.915	0.75	2.76
Rice	—	0.1	0.890	0.934	0.75	4.39
Other Crops	—	0.4	1.400	1.359	0.93	2.32
Edible Oils	0.057	0.4	1.800	1.730	12.86	29.7
Other Foods	0.110	0.2	1.150	1.132	0.64	3.22
Textiles	0.188	0.2	1.300	1.255	1.23	5.53
Consumer goods	0.211	0.2	1.270	1.248	0.56	2.68
Durables	0.679	0.6	1.870	1.716	25.49	42.12

a.   This is the ratio of domestic to border price.

The price ratio that would prevail in the absence of rationing and if imports were perfect substitutes for domestic production is one plus the tariff rate. The difference between this and the observed NPC is due to imperfect substitutability and import rationing. By removing import rationing, the price ratio should decrease, but not go below one plus the tariff rate. Similar changes are expected for export rationing. To illustrate how the price and trade changes observed differ for different values of the export rationing factor (k), these changes in the case of rice (for which there is no export tax) are shown for $k = 0.1$ and $k = 0.2$. Thus, the price difference when rationing is removed falls from 0.11 to 0.085 (when $k = 0.2$) and the export ratio increases from 0.75 per cent to 2.76 per cent. If $k = 0.1$, the price difference falls to 0.066 and the export ratio goes up to 4.39 per cent[11]. For commodities that have high import ratios to start with, both the price and the import ratio after removal of rationing have to be examined. Thus for edible oils and fats, the removal of rationing leads to only a small decline in domestic price (from 1.8 to 1.73 times world price), but a large increase in the share of imports in absorption to almost 30 per cent. Though the decrease in price is small any larger increase in imports was thought to be improbably large and the rationing parameter was not decreased any further.

2.6 The Labour Market

How urban and rural labour markets adjust under changes in prices and labour demands is of crucial importance for changes in income distribution and welfare and for the outcome of adjustment policies[12]. There are major institutional differences between rural and urban labour markets. The rural labour market is largely unorganised and wages and employment can be expected to adjust rapidly to changes in demand or supply. Large segments of the urban labour market, on the other hand, are organised, and labour mobility between sectors is lower and the adjustment process slower than in agriculture.

The effects on income distribution and welfare of price changes clearly depend on assumptions about labour markets. For example, if the nominal rural wage is fixed, increased food prices will result in a shift in the rural income distribution, with the landless losing and surplus producers gaining. In addition to affecting distributional outcomes, as Hertel (1990) points out in his survey of models of trade liberalisation, assumptions about labour markets can also be crucial in determining whether agricultural liberalisation improves overall welfare in developing countries.

In the context of CGE modelling, it is worthwhile to distinguish between labour market adjustment in the short, medium and long run. In an economy with a small formal sector it is plausible that in the short run nominal wages are fixed and an increase in the general price level results in a decrease in real wages. However, this cannot be implemented in a purely real CGE model without money because in such a model the price level is not endogenous and the nominal wage cannot be fixed — fixing the nominal wage really amounts to fixing the wage relative to the numéraire, and if the numéraire is the price index, the real wage. In the medium run, wages are assumed to be sensitive to the price of food. If the price of food goes up (relative to that of other commodities), the wage goes up with an elasticity of 0.5 (estimated by Ahluwalia, 1985). Since the general price index is taken to be the numéraire, this translates into an increase in the real wage, i.e. in the wage divided by the general price index. The argument here is that wages are more sensitive to food prices than to other prices, but that wages do not adjust completely to increases in food prices. Lastly, in the long run wages are determined by market clearing with a labour supply that responds to real wages with an elasticity of 0.3, as in Binswanger and Quizon (1986)[13]. These assumptions apply to both rural and urban labour markets. In addition, the two labour markets function independently, i.e. rural-urban migration is ignored. There are two reasons for this choice: the lack of good econometric models of migration behaviour and the fact that migration is an issue which should be considered in conjunction with other long-term concerns such as accumulation and productivity growth, which are not a central feature of this study.

Notes and References

1. Because the agricultural supply and input demand model does not distinguish between hired and family labour, payments to family labour are imputed using the same wage rate as is used for hired labour and the two are combined to give total payments to labour.

2. De Janvry and Subbarao based the distribution of agricultural incomes in their SAM on a study by Ali *et al.* (1980), which used data from the Agricultural Census for 1976 and the National Sample Survey of 1974-75. In defining the rural household classes I have had to assume that the distribution of land did not change and that population growth rates in each class are the same as that for the rural population as a whole.

3. Exports and imports are taken to be policy variables. Government can raise taxes, but they are assumed to be spent in such a way as not to affect agricultural supply or demand.

4. Because of the significant differences across regions in agroclimatic conditions, technology, price responsiveness, production costs and rates of commercialisation, changes in policy are likely to have regionally uneven impacts. A regionally disaggregated model of agriculture would be required to examine this issue. Such a model was not developed here because the data requirements for a regional SAM are substantial and not easily fulfilled.

5. This is equivalent to assuming that the capital-to-labour ratio in the informal sector is the same as that in the formal sector and that the self-employed receive both wages and gross profits.

6. The reason the original parameter estimates were not used is that the elasticities came from several studies for different agroclimatic regions and were aggregated by Binswanger and Quizon to obtain elasticities for the entire country.

7. The transfer to households is the quantity of ration sales times the difference between the ration price and the open market price. This is not the same as the benefit to households from the food subsidy scheme, which is the difference between what they pay now and what they would have paid had their been no ration sales. It is this latter figure for which George (1988) provides an estimate.

8. These budget shares are obtained from disaggregated estimates of private consumption in the national accounts and are taken to be the same for all household groups.

9. Restrictions on exports are similarly treated.

10. As Dervis *et al.* note, rationing forces consumers off their demand curves for the import and the composite commodity and in principle one should solve the consumers' constrained maximisation problem. The simpler formulation used here assumes that consumers are still on their demand curves for the composite good. They point out that this simplification is not likely to be a problem for producer goods, which are demanded in fixed proportions, but not for consumer goods. Since most of India's imports are of producer goods, this treatment is justifiable.

11. These ratios are not extraordinarily high; exports in 1981-82, for example, were almost five times their level in 1983-84, the base year for the model.

12. The success of trade liberalisation and structural adjustment hinges upon transferring resources from sectors which are no longer protected to sectors which are no longer taxed. Urban labour market performance is clearly a major determinant of the outcome. In this context, it should be noted that the reforms currently under way in India mark a major shift in policy because they explicitly endorse the idea of reducing employment in loss-making firms in the public sector. To enhance labour mobility and provide short-term compensation, the government plans to set up a worker compensation and retraining fund. However, opposition to the idea of large-scale reductions in public sector employment has come not only from workers' unions and opposition parties, but also from within the ruling party.

13. The long run is interpreted here as a time period over which the effects of capital accumulation and productivity growth are unimportant, but by the end of which full employment prevails. Of course, the notion of full employment in a labour-surplus economy is problematic. While several studies (see Binswanger and Rosenzweig for a collection of such studies) have established that rural wages are sensitive to market forces, this does not negate the finding that surplus labour exists.

Chapter 3

Scenarios for Policy Reforms

Government intervention has had an uneven impact on Indian agriculture. The combination of restrictions on trade, interventions in output markets and subsidies on inputs has resulted in a high degree of protection for some crops and some degree of taxation for other crops. The recent economic crisis in India has forced policy-makers to confront the issues of trade liberalisation and reduction in subsidies. At the same time, liberalisation of agricultural trade by the OECD countries is expected to result in higher world agricultural prices, which can significantly affect the outcome of domestic policy reforms. These possibilities are explored using three sets of scenarios. The first set revolves around agricultural trade liberalisation in India without and with higher world agricultural prices. The second set of scenarios concentrates on domestic policy issues, such as possible responses to exogenous increases in crop yields and reduction in fertilizer subsidy. The third set of scenarios is concerned with food subsidy policy. In interpreting the results from these simulations it should be borne in mind that the impact of changes in domestic policy or in world prices can be extremely uneven across agroclimatic regions in India. This unevenness results from differences across regions in cropping patterns, degree of commercialisation, level of state intervention, and level of infrastructural development and transport costs to ports. Consequently, what appear to be minor changes in income at the all-India level might well mask substantial losses in some regions which are counterbalanced by gains in other regions. It may be possible in some cases to draw upon existing studies and provide some qualitative indications about regional impacts, but quantitative results will require the development of a regional model.

As noted above, two assumptions about the labour market are used. Under the first, unemployment exists, rural and urban labour markets do not clear and rural and urban (real) wages adjust partially to changes in the food price index with an elasticity of 0.5. Full employment is the second assumption used. It should be noted, however, that the simulations assume complete labour mobility within agriculture and within industry, which is unrealistic. Consequently, some of the changes may be understated and others overstated. Changes in employment will be smaller and changes in value added and profits larger than those predicted by the model. In addition, as the earlier discussion on labour markets notes, labour market adjustment is likely to proceed faster in agriculture than in industry. This difference in adjustment speeds will matter most when liberalisation is extended to industry[1].

Another important consideration in these simulations is the need to prevent expansion fuelled by foreign borrowing because foreign borrowing has no short-run cost in a model of this type[2]. So the balance of payments is kept fixed and the exchange rate is allowed to adjust. In addition, except in scenarios where food procurement and subsidy policy is the focus, I keep government procurement and subsidised sales of wheat and rice constant so that the building up or drawing down of government food stocks do not confuse the picture. I also assume that investment is determined by savings; consequentially, changes in household, government or foreign savings are reflected in changes in investment[3].

Scenarios 1, 2 and 3 examine the impact of agricultural trade liberalisation in India and of higher world food prices arising from trade liberalisation by the OECD countries. The first of these traces the effects of trade liberalisation by India at current world prices, i.e. in the absence of world-wide trade liberalisation[4]. Two possibilities arise in this scenario. Under the first, only trade in unprocessed commodities is liberalised, while under the second, trade in edible oils, sugar and other (processed) foods is also liberalised. These can have very different implications for welfare, domestic prices and trade because of the very different levels of protection and taxation afforded the crop and food processing sectors, because of differences in trade shares and degree of price transmission, because of the strong linkages between these sectors and because of the large share of food in the household budget.

Moreover, the political implications of the two kinds of liberalisation are likely to be different. Liberalisation of agricultural processing is likely to arouse strong opposition for three reasons. Firstly, much of the agricultural processing sector is in urban areas and in the organised sector, where protests are easier to organise[5]. Secondly, the level of protection for agricultural processing is often large and the losses from liberalisation may be too substantial to be swallowed meekly. Thirdly, reduction of protection for agricultural processing will doubtless put pressure on input prices and reduce the level of protection for agricultural inputs and therefore face opposition from farm interests also[6]. In agriculture, on the other hand, except for some crops, notably oilseeds, the level of protection is small, and in any case, the removal of protection for these crops may be acceptable as part of a larger package that eliminates taxation as well as protection. However, the regional impact of liberalisation can be quite uneven and those farmers who stand to lose from removal of protection may not be the same as those who expect to gain from removal of taxation. Without further modelling to identify winners and losers and the amounts involved, the relative strengths of farmer opposition to or support for agricultural trade liberalisation cannot be judged.

Scenario 2 takes trade liberalisation a step further. Non-agricultural trade is also liberalised. Given the large share of non-food items in imports and exports (89 per cent and 84 per cent, respectively in 1983-84), the relatively high trade ratios in some non-food sectors, and the generally higher level of industrial protection the impact of non-agricultural trade liberalisation will clearly overwhelm that of agricultural trade liberalisation for the economy as a whole[7].

Scenario 3 examines the implications for India of the higher world agricultural prices that are expected to result following agricultural trade liberalisation by the OECD countries under GATT. Three variants are examined. In the first, agricultural exports and imports do not change, i.e. no attempt is made to adjust to the changed prices. Given the small share of India's agricultural exports and imports in total trade in the base year, doing nothing in response to higher prices cannot be ruled out, at least in the short run. In the second variant, India's agricultural trade is also liberalised, i.e. tariffs and other trade restrictions are withdrawn. Finally, in the last variant, tariffs and other restrictions on non-agricultural trade are also removed.

The second set of scenarios focuses on domestic interventions in agriculture. Scenario 4 considers crop-specific increases in productivity under different trade and domestic procurement and food subsidy policies. Trade policy and domestic intervention through government procurement can substantially alter the distribution of gains from an increase in agricultural production. In addition, the impact of increased productivity and of the different policy responses will differ substantially from crop to crop because of differences in trade ratios, in consumption and input-output linkages and in existing interventions.

Scenario 5 addresses the implications of cutting the fertilizer subsidy. As seen above, agriculture-related subsidies have shot up over the last decade and are now a major concern for structural adjustment[8]. It should be borne in mind, however, that the fertilizer subsidy scheme is far more complex than is modelled here (see, for example, Gulati and Sharma, 1990a). The scheme involves subsidies for storage of imported fertilizer and for transport, and plant-specific subsidies for producers, based on cost and production norms, none of which are modelled here. Moreover, the regional impact will be quite uneven because of the wide variation in intensity of fertilizer use and therefore in incidence of subsidy[9].

Scenarios similar to these were studied by Binswanger and Quizon using a linearised general equilibrium model with an exogenous non-agricultural sector. A comparison with their results is interesting because it shows that important qualitative changes take place when the exogenous non-agricultural sector is replaced with an endogenous, fully specified non-agricultural sector.

The operation of the food procurement and subsidy programme is studied in Scenarios 6 and 7. Scenario 6A examines the gains from the programme by simulating the outcome when procurement and subsidised sales are discontinued. Scenario 6B considers the effects of increasing procurement by 5 per cent and increasing sales correspondingly. Scenario 7 simulates changes in the targeting of food subsidies, which in the base year are assumed to reach only urban worker and marginal households.

Several of the scenarios outlined above involve significant changes in government revenues or expenditures. Policies which result in large reductions in revenues will hardly recommend themselves to government if unaccompanied by measures to increase revenue from other sources. Similarly, increased expenditure on subsidies will have to be met by increasing revenues. Thus in the domestic trade liberalisation scenarios, the indirect tax rate is adjusted to offset the decrease in tariff revenues and maintain revenue neutrality. Domestic liberalisation is an explicit policy and can therefore be combined with measures to enhance non-tariff revenues to compensate for loss of tariff revenues. But an increase in world agricultural prices is exogenous and not the result of domestic policy, and the effects of this change on government finances are themselves of interest. Revenue-neutrality is therefore not insisted upon in the world agricultural liberalisation scenarios, where it is assumed that pre-existing tax rates stay in place. In the food subsidy scenarios, the increase in expenditure is matched by an increase in tax revenue, i.e. government savings are kept constant. On the other hand, in the fertilizer subsidy scenario, the reduction in subsidy is not offset by a decrease in government revenues on the grounds that a decrease in the government deficit is desirable[10].

1. Agricultural Liberalisation in India

This scenario simulates the effects of removing all tariffs and restrictions on agricultural trade. These restrictions include government monopoly over imports, export bans, quotas and licensing requirements. These restrictions are modelled by assuming that the actual trade ratio is kept at a level below the desired trade ratio. With the removal of restrictions the actual and desired trade ratios coincide. Two possibilities are considered. In Scenario 1A, trade in unprocessed commodities — rice, wheat, coarse cereals and other crops — is liberalised. In the other (1B), trade in processed commodities (edible oils, sugar and other foods) is also liberalised. In these cases and in the scenarios on domestic liberalisation which follow, indirect taxes on non-agricultural commodities are changed in order to keep government revenues constant[11].

When trade in the unprocessed crops is liberalised (Table 15), the major changes are that rice exports increase almost six-fold and other crops imports increase some 230 per cent. The price of rice increases by 3.1 per cent and that for other crops falls 2.8 per cent. The net effect on agriculture is small, the prices of wheat and coarse cereals change hardly at all, and agricultural value added increases by 0.12 per cent under partial adjustment of wages and falls by 0.45 per cent under full employment. The agro-processing sectors expand because the price of other crops, a major input for these sectors, falls as imports increase[12]. All other non-agricultural sectors also expand and as is to be expected, their expansion is weaker under full employment. Under partially adjusting wages, GDP increases 0.77 per cent, real incomes of all rural groups increase by 0.5 per cent to 0.6 per cent and real incomes of all urban groups by 1 per cent to 1.3 per cent. The increase for the urban groups is higher because non-agriculture expands more than agriculture. Urban and rural wages are higher under full employment, agricultural value added decreases and non-agricultural expansion is weaker, so GDP growth is only 0.29 per cent. The landless gain as much as before because total agricultural wages go up more under full employment, and the gains for all other rural classes are much smaller. Urban incomes rise by 0.63 per cent to 0.84 per cent.

When trade in processed commodities is also liberalised, the changes are larger because exports, imports, prices and output of edible oils, sugar and other processed foods change substantially, which then has repercussions on agriculture and on the group-specific food price indices. Edible oil imports double, the price falls by 5.3 per cent (the producer price by 3.8 per cent) and production by 13 per cent. Sugar exports fall by half and imports of other foods go up over four-fold[13]. The prices of all these commodities fall, wheat and rice prices go up, and the price of other crops falls more than in Scenario 1A because of the contraction of the agro-processing sectors. As a result, agricultural value added falls by 0.31 per cent, unlike in Scenario 1A, where it rose by 0.12 per cent. Under full employment, agricultural wages increase by 0.63 per cent rather than decreasing 0.18 per cent as they do here under partial wage adjustment

44

and agricultural value added falls 1.8 per cent. Under partial adjustment, the non-agricultural, non-processing sectors expand by 2 per cent to 4 per cent. This falls to 0.5 per cent to 2.5 per cent under full employment because wages are higher.

Under partial adjustment of wages, GDP increases by 1.5 per cent and rural incomes by 1 per cent to 1.7 per cent, even though agricultural value added decreases, the reason being that non-agricultural incomes increase substantially, more than making up for the decrease in agricultural incomes. As a result of the non-agricultural expansion, urban incomes increase by 2.5 per cent to 3.2 per cent. Under full employment, GDP increases only 0.22 per cent, agricultural value added falls by 1.8 per cent and large farmers lose 0.36 per cent of their base-year real income, while gains of medium farmers are only 0.05 per cent. Urban incomes increase only 1.6 per cent to 1.9 per cent because of the weaker non-agricultural expansion.

The increase in agricultural imports (including processed commodities) in Scenario 1B is more than twice as high as in Scenario 1A, while the increase in agricultural exports is only some 25 per cent higher. A larger increase in non-agricultural exports is required in Scenario 1B to pay for the increased imports. Hence, in Scenario 1B the currency depreciates by 3.6 per cent as opposed to 0.3 per cent in Scenario 1A (under partial adjustment of wages). In both Scenarios 1A and 1B, the effect on government revenue is minimal because tariff income in the base year from agriculture and processed agricultural commodities is small and because non-agricultural expansion increases government's profit income. In fact, small reductions of the order of 0.01 per cent to 0.2 per cent in indirect tax rates are required to keep government revenues at their old level.

In both scenarios, agricultural trade liberalisation does not improve agricultural income, except in Scenario 1A in the medium run, because the overall effect of trade interventions is small. As the comparison between Scenarios 1A and 1B shows, liberalisation of trade in processed agricultural commodities can have adverse effects on agriculture even if trade in unprocessed commodities is also liberalised. There are two reasons why this happens. Firstly, the processing sectors are highly protected and liberalisation results in large decreases in output and derived demand for the agricultural inputs. Secondly, liberalisation of trade in unprocessed commodities alone cannot provide a strong stimulus to agriculture because, as was argued above in Chapter 1, Section 5, the net protection or taxation afforded agriculture by direct interventions in agriculture is small. However, lacking data which would permit disaggregating the other crops aggregate in the model and data on NPCs for all the crops in this aggregate — some of which are protected and others taxed — any conclusions about this commodity group must be treated with caution.

The basic results are not very sensitive to choice of assumptions about the labour market. Wages are higher and employment lower under full employment than with wages that are tied to food prices because the food price index decreases in both scenarios (except in Scenario 1A, where the rural wage increases slightly); even though cereal prices go up, other food prices decline even further. As a result, the increase in non-agricultural value added is smaller and the decrease in agricultural value added larger under full employment. As is to be expected, the adverse effects on agriculture of liberalisation of trade in processed agricultural commodities are more pronounced under full employment.

2. Liberalisation of Trade in all Commodities

In Scenario 2 all tariffs are set to zero and all trade rationing is removed[14]. The result is to increase imports and exports that had earlier been taxed or restricted. The change in export or import levels depends on the size of the tariff or the degree of rationing that was removed, the elasticity of transformation between domestic sales and exports or the elasticity of substitution between domestic production and imports and the extent of devaluation. Since non-agricultural tariffs are heavier and non-agricultural imports predominate, the decrease in tariff revenue is large and has to be offset by an increase in indirect taxes, which are increased by the same absolute amount in all non-agricultural sectors. The most significant changes (see Table 15) are in sectors where rationing is removed and where there are large tariffs. A 26.8 per cent devaluation is required to restore external balance when all tariffs and trade restrictions are removed[15]. Large increases in trade occur in rice, wheat, other crops, edible oils, other processed foods, clothing, consumer goods, durables. The increases for consumer goods and clothing are from low initial values. The initial tariffs in some sectors are lower than the devaluation, so in these sectors imports fall after liberalisation. Relative prices within agriculture change substantially; rice and wheat prices increase by 15.4 per cent and 10.9 per cent because the trade shares for these are significant, the price of coarse cereals goes up by 3.2 per cent as consumers substitute away from other cereals, and the price of other crops falls slightly because of the opposing effects of devaluation and removal of tariffs. Value added in agriculture increases by 6.6 per cent. Agricultural wages move up 2.6 per cent as food prices go up and agricultural employment increases slightly, by 0.28 per cent.

Non-agricultural wages increase much less, by 0.71 per cent, because the weight of cereals in the food price index for urban workers is small. Non-agricultural employment and value added fall 7 per cent. All non-agricultural sectors except fertilizer contract. Value added in these sectors falls by 4 per cent to 7 per cent, except in edible oils and durables, where it falls 13 per cent and 22 per cent. In the case of durables, the decrease is large because of the large increase in imports after liberalisation and the large trade ratio, which results in a large price transmission coefficient. In the case of edible oils, imports increase because of removal of the quota on imports, but the market price increases at the same time because of the large devaluation. Demand decreases and output decreases further because of the increased imports and the producer price actually falls. As a result, value added per unit in edible oils falls around 6 per cent. The increase in fertilizer import price causes users to substitute toward domestic production. Price increases 10 per cent and value added 18 per cent.

GDP decreases 3.2 per cent and only large farmers gain. All rural nominal incomes increase because the large increase in agricultural value added more than counterbalances the decrease in rural non-agricultural income. But because of the increase in food prices, real incomes decrease for all but large farmers, who gain 1.6 per cent, while the landless and medium farmers lose about 1.5 per cent and small farmers lose 3 per cent. Because liberalisation causes the terms of trade to move in favour of agriculture by 5 per cent and because of non-agricultural contraction, all urban incomes fall by 6.1 per cent to 7.3 per cent.

Under full employment, the major change is that the non-agricultural wage falls because demand for non-agricultural labour decreases, while the increase in agricultural labour demand causes agricultural wages to increase further. As a result, non-agricultural output is higher and agricultural output lower than in the medium run and the terms of trade move further in favour of agriculture, producing a larger increase in agricultural value added. Of course, under full employment the decrease in GDP is small, only 0.15 per cent. Because of the large increase in agricultural value added and larger increase in food prices, rural incomes are higher than before, but the landless and small farmers continue to be losers, while large farmers make sizeable gains. All urban classes lose by 3.4 per cent to 4.1 per cent.

Comparing Scenarios 1A, 1B and 2, it is clear that agriculture does better when trade liberalisation is extended to non-agricultural commodities. Under Scenario 2, the price of rice and wheat go up further and the price and output decline noted for other crops under Scenario 1B is restrained. The 26 per cent devaluation in Scenario 2 means that the effect of removing protection to other crops (and to sectors using other crops as input, such as edible oils, sugar and other foods) is diminished and that exports increase from this sector.

Since food prices go up and subsidised sales prices stay the same, the consumer subsidy increases by 82 per cent (97 per cent in the full employment case), but the outlay by government on food subsidy and buffer stock operations (which depends on the difference between procurement price and subsidised sale price) decreases by 7.8 per cent (0.42 per cent with full employment) because with the increase in production, the decrease in procurement costs for rice outweighs the increase in procurement costs for wheat.

Confining trade liberalisation to agriculture and processed agricultural commodities is clearly inadequate for increasing agricultural incomes. By extending liberalisation to all other sectors, the implicit taxation of agriculture caused by overvaluation of the exchange rate is reversed and agricultural value added rises significantly. However, the gains in agriculture are concentrated in the hands of the large farmer class. The landless and small farmers lose because the increase in food prices outweighs the increase in their nominal incomes. The gains are larger (and losses smaller) in the long run because full employment prevails.

Since government revenues are maintained constant and total subsidies fall, government savings increase. Total savings and investment remain stable or increase slightly because the decrease in household savings is compensated for by the increase in government savings and the large increase in foreign savings resulting from the devaluation.

3. Liberalisation of World Agricultural Trade

Scenario 3 considers the effects of increased world prices for agricultural products on the Indian economy[16]. Several possibilities are considered. The first (3A) is a do-nothing scenario: world prices increase, but India's trade in agricultural commodities remains unchanged; no attempt is made to adjust to the change in world prices and the burden of adjustment falls on the non-agricultural sectors. In the other two scenarios (3B and 3C) the concern is with the effect of higher world agricultural prices when India liberalises agricultural and non-agricultural trade. In Scenario 3B, tariffs and trade restrictions on all agricultural products are withdrawn and in Scenario 3C, all trade is liberalised. Thus Scenarios 3B and 3C correspond to Scenarios 1B and 2, but with higher world agricultural prices. Since higher world prices are superimposed, so to speak, on these domestic liberalisation scenarios the same changes in tax rates are used here as in these scenarios, i.e. liberalisation would be revenue-neutral if world food prices were not to change.

In Scenario 3A, when world food prices increase and India's trade in food commodities does not change, the impact on the economy is slight, as the results in Table 16 show. Both agricultural imports and exports increase by about 20 per cent, and since agricultural exports exceed agricultural imports to start with, this causes a slight currency appreciation. But since agricultural trade is a minor part of total trade (the share of agricultural commodities in exports is 13.9 per cent and in imports 10.4 per cent), the change in world prices has little impact on the economy. Prices change hardly at all and GDP increases 0.01 per cent under full employment and 0.08 per cent when wages adjust partially to food prices.

In Scenario 3B, trade shares tend to be larger because of liberalisation of trade, hence price transmission is larger and net exports in agriculture increase strongly, leading to currency appreciation by 4.3 per cent. However, in sectors such as other crops, edible oils and sugar the combined effect of liberalisation and higher world prices is such as to leave domestic prices almost unchanged. The major changes are in sectors which were not protected before — rice and wheat — prices of which increases by 10.9 per cent and 5.8 per cent, respectively. The terms of trade move in favour of agriculture by 3.8 per cent, agriculture expands by 4.9 per cent and non-agriculture contracts by 1.3 per cent. Unlike Scenario 1B, in which only the agro-processing sectors contracted, here all non-agricultural sectors except fertilizers contract. As a result, the increase in non-tariff revenues is smaller than in Scenario 1B and is not enough to maintain government revenue constant. Government revenue falls 2.7 per cent, investment 3.1 per cent and GDP increases only 0.41 per cent. The sectoral effects are as would be expected, large farmers are the major gainers, their incomes go up 3 per cent, and medium farmers gain 1.28 per cent. All others lose 0.5 per cent to 1.2 per cent of their incomes. With full employment the results are similar. Agricultural wages are higher and non-agricultural wages lower because agricultural labour demand increases and non-agricultural labour demand decreases. Agricultural output is lower and non-agricultural output higher. Hence the terms of trade move further in favour of agriculture, large and medium farmers gain, other classes' losses increase slightly and GDP increases 0.84 per cent.

Comparing Scenario 1B and 3B, when there is full employment, higher world agricultural prices result in higher GDP, as would be expected for a net exporter of agricultural commodities. Instead of full employment, when wages are assumed to be "sticky" and tied to food prices, higher food prices are contractionary because they result in higher wages. This suggests that in the medium run, when wages are sticky, higher world food prices are contractionary, but in the longer run, when wages are determined by market clearing, the economy stands to gain from higher world prices. But higher world food prices while increasing aggregate income also change income distribution. Without higher world food prices, liberalisation of agricultural trade produced losses for large farmers and gains for the other classes because the gains from higher prices for taxed crops are outweighed by the losses from lower prices for processed agricultural commodities. With higher food prices, this is reversed because prices for processed commodities do not fall as much and crop prices increase further, and large and medium farmers stand to gain and others to lose.

In Scenario 3C, higher world food prices follow in the wake of complete liberalisation. In Scenario 2 (complete liberalisation), devaluation and removal of trade restrictions resulted in large increases in agricultural prices and decreases in non-agricultural prices, with the terms of trade moving in favour of agriculture by 5 per cent in the medium run (sticky wages) and 9 per cent in the long run (full employment). Now with higher world food prices superimposed, domestic agricultural prices move up further. With sticky wages (i.e. in the medium run) the terms of trade improve by 10.5 per cent, rice prices increase 24 per cent and wheat prices 14 per cent and agricultural value added increases 13 per cent as opposed to 6.6 per cent in Scenario 2. Agricultural net exports increase more than in Scenario 2 because of the higher world food prices and a smaller devaluation is required to maintain the balance of trade constant. As a result, non-agricultural imports increase more and prices, value added and employment fall further than in Scenario 2. GDP decreases further and as in Scenario 2, the only gainers are large farmers. Urban real incomes decline by 9.2 per cent to 11.4 per cent.

With full employment, i.e. in the long run, the non-agricultural labour market adjusts, non-agricultural wages fall substantially and the decrease in output is smaller; as a result non-agricultural prices fall further and the terms of trade change in favour of agriculture by 17 per cent. Agricultural value added increases 19 per cent, rice and wheat prices by 27.6 per cent and 18.7 per cent, and agricultural wages by 5.7 per cent. GDP increases by 0.51 per cent as opposed to the small loss of 0.15 per cent in Scenario 2. As is to be expected, large farmers gain substantially, by 9.5 per cent, followed by medium farmers, who gain 3 per cent, while all other classes lose.

4. Technical Change

In this scenario crop yields increase by 10 per cent as a result of neutral technical change[17]. The effects on prices, incomes and income distribution depend critically on whether or not external trade is allowed to adjust and by how much. Thus when rice yield increases by 10 per cent (Scenario 4A, Column 1, Table 17), the price drops by 13 per cent, imports by 83 per cent and exports go up by 270 per cent (282 per cent under full employment), a consequence of the assumed high elasticities of substitution between domestic sales and exports (ten) and domestic production and imports (fifteen)[18]. Since rice prices fall substantially, the food price index decreases and real wages decline somewhat. The net result is that value added in crop agriculture decreases by 0.9 per cent and profits by 0.74 per cent (2.0 per cent and 2.3 per cent, respectively, under full employment). Value added in the non-crop sectors increases by 1 to 4 per cent and urban incomes by 1.4 per cent to 2.2 per cent. Income of capitalists increases the most in relative terms because (real) wages decline and non-agricultural output increases[19]. Rural household agricultural wage incomes decrease by 1 per cent while their non-agricultural income increases. The landless and small farmers gain the most because the decline in food prices helps them the most, i.e. the largest decreases in the group-specific price indices are for these households. Gains of large farmers are smallest. Under full employment, agricultural wages fall only slightly while non-agricultural wages increase because of increased non-agricultural labour demand. The terms of trade move further against agriculture and large farmer real incomes fall about 0.5 per cent. The major difference between the outcomes under full employment and under partial adjustment of wages is that under the latter, wages fall in response to food price decreases and so the outcome is more expansionary.

GDP increases by 1.3 per cent (0.38 per cent under full employment). Government savings increase partly because of the decrease of over 40 per cent in the food subsidy bill. As a result, investment increases sharply by 5 per cent (3.2 per cent under full employment). The exchange rate appreciates by 0.06 per cent under full employment because production of rice, a tradable, increases. Under partial adjustment of wages, the expansion is larger and hence imports increase further, requiring a depreciation of 0.28 per cent to produce a corresponding increase in exports to maintain the balance of payments constant. Labour demand in agriculture increases by only 0.72 per cent even though real agricultural wages, being indexed to food prices, decrease by 1.8 per cent. And under full employment, agricultural employment changes hardly at all.

In Scenario 4B, all agricultural trade is kept constant as if there were fixed quotas in effect. The price of rice decreases by 15 per cent (16 per cent under full employment, where the expansion of demand is smaller). Because of crop substitution in production and increased demand, prices and output for wheat and other crops increase. The price of coarse cereals falls by 1.8 per cent because demand is inelastic. The decline in real wages is larger and non-crop sectors see greater expansion. Again, though the agricultural wage bill decreases, the landless and small farmers gain because of increased non-agricultural income and the decrease in food prices. As before, the non-agricultural classes gain from low food prices and large farmers stand to lose. Since the decrease in rice price is larger than in Scenario 4A, large farmers lose more, 1.5 per cent under full employment and 0.17 per cent under partial adjustment of wages.

In these scenarios, the increase in rice output is equivalent to an increase of 0.5 per cent in GDP (at base-year prices) and GDP increases by about 1.23 per cent in Scenario 4A, suggesting an agriculture-industry multiplier of about 1.4[20]. A comparison with Binswanger and Quizon's results is instructive. Assuming full employment and no change in trade, they found a much larger gain of about 4 per cent in GDP for a 20 per cent increase in rice yield, whereas GDP increases here by 0.28 per cent for a 10 per cent increase in yield. In their simulation the price of rice declined by 31 per cent, i.e. 15.5 per cent for a 10 per cent yield increase, which is similar to the producer price decrease of 15.7 per cent found here. The other point where Binswanger-Quizon's results differ is in the implications for labour demand: they find an increase of 0.55 per cent; here a decrease of 0.26 per cent is observed[21]. In their simulation, GDP increases so sharply because all agricultural prices fall substantially, not just the price of rice. In the simulation reported here, the very opposite occurs and other agricultural prices increase slightly. The reason for this difference may lie in the fact that the agricultural supply parameters used here differ slightly from those used by them, but since the own-price supply elasticities are the same, it seems unlikely that differences in cross-price elasticities should be responsible for the difference in behaviour. Another reason could be that they use a demand system which differs considerably from the one used here.

Another possibility is that exports of rice can be treated as a policy variable — given the level of state intervention in foreign trade it may be more sensible to take trade in agricultural commodities to be exogenous, i.e. the government decides how much to import or export depending on domestic and world market conditions. In Scenarios 4B1 and 4B2, all agricultural exports and imports are kept fixed and exports of rice are increased by 4 per cent and 6 per cent of the base-year level of production, which is equivalent to an increase in exports by factors of 8 and 12 over the base-year level. Such an increase is not unrealistic, going by past performance of rice exports. The price of rice falls by 10.3 per cent and 7.3 per cent and output increases by 9.5 per cent and 11.3 per cent respectively. GDP increases by 1.05 per cent and 0.89 per cent, as opposed to 1.32 per cent in Scenario 4B, where no change in exports took place[22]. Again, the higher the price of rice, the larger the gains to medium and large farmers and the smaller the gains to net buyers of food — the landless, small farmers and the urban classes. Indeed, when rice exports increase by 6 per cent of base-year output, the effect on many non-agricultural sectors is contractionary because of the currency appreciation caused by the increase in exports and urban classes do not gain at all. These results are not sensitive to the labour market specification and similar changes are observed under full employment.

A third possibility is that the government may use procurement policy to support rice prices. The increase in rice yields increases GDP and therefore government revenue and depresses rice prices and thereby reduces the food subsidy, which makes it possible for the government to procure more rice without having to cut back other expenditures. In Scenario 4B3, the rice procurement price is raised some 17 per cent. Procurement of rice goes up by 20 per cent, i.e. about 2.4 per cent of initial production, and the extra rice procured is sold to the consumer at the same subsidised price as before. Compared to Scenario 4A, the producer price of rice rises 3.3 per cent (2.6 per cent under full employment). In the medium run, agricultural value added and the rural classes' nominal incomes are higher than in Scenario 4A. But the increase in food prices translates into lower real incomes for the landless and small farmers, with some small gains only for the large farmers. Urban classes, including the recipients of the increased food subsidy, lose because the increase in non-agricultural value added is smaller than in Scenario 4A. In the long run, the results are similar. The increase in rice procurement results in a smaller decrease in agricultural value added, a smaller increase in non-agricultural value added, and higher rural nominal incomes, but real incomes are higher only for medium and large farmers. However, government procurement as a means of securing higher incomes for the agricultural sector is not as effective as is recourse to trade. In Scenario 4B2, where rice exports are allowed to increase by 4 per cent of base year output, the incomes for all rural households except the landless are higher than in the current scenario, the landless are only slightly worse off and the increase in investment is 3.4 per cent above the base year's level as opposed to 0.7 per cent in the procurement scenario.

When wheat yields increase by 10 per cent (Scenario 4C), the results are similar with an important difference. The base-year import ratio for wheat is substantially higher at 7.8 per cent so that the decrease of 51 per cent observed in imports accounts for about 40 per cent of the increase in wheat output. The price of wheat decreases less sharply (about 9 per cent) so the gains are more evenly distributed than when rice yields increased in Scenario 4A. And since wheat's share in output is smaller than that of rice, the expansionary effect is smaller.

In the case of a yield increase for coarse cereals (Scenario 4D), another factor comes into play. Not only is external trade insignificant, but the expenditure elasticity is smaller than for rice and wheat, so that domestic demand is a weaker influence[23]. Since the share of coarse cereals in total output is smaller than that of the other crops, the expansionary effect is weaker and GDP increases 0.18 per cent (under partial adjustment of wages). The price of coarse cereals falls by 15 per cent and agricultural wage income and profits decrease. Large farmers' incomes decline slightly and the other rural classes' incomes increase because of the large decline in the price of coarse cereals, the budget share of which is high in rural areas. Urban wages do not change because coarse cereals are unimportant in urban budgets. Urban incomes increase because of the increase in non-agricultural activity.

The other crops aggregate (Scenario 4E) provides several interesting contrasts. Firstly, this is a large sector, accounting for over half of agricultural output, so that the observed 8.9 per cent increase in production is about 1.2 per cent of GDP. Secondly, it has strong linkages to agricultural processing sectors in industry, such as edible oils, sugar, other foods and textiles, which are tradables and which have elastic domestic demand. As a result, production and exports of these commodities increase. Demand for other commodities also goes up substantially because of consumption and investment demand linkages. Because of these linkages to other sectors, domestic demand increases substantially so that the price of other crops decreases by only 11.2 per cent. All household groups find their incomes increase, but urban incomes increase substantially more than do rural incomes because of the large shift of 5.4 per cent in the terms of trade and the large non-agricultural expansion. GDP increases by 4.7 per cent and investment by 12 per cent. Under full employment, the non-agricultural expansion is weaker, the price of other crops falls further and the terms of trade move against agriculture by 8.3 per cent. The increase in rural and urban incomes is smaller and incomes of large farmers actually decline by 1.1 per cent.

Finally, in Scenario 4F, when all crop yields increase by 10 per cent (i.e. 2.8 per cent of GDP at base year prices), GDP increases by 6.8 per cent. All real incomes go up, the smallest gains are to the large farmers and the biggest to urban marginal and capitalist households. The reason is that all crop prices decline, so that wages (which are indexed to food prices) fall, input costs for agricultural processing industries fall, demand increases and profits increase. The changes in crop exports, imports and production do not differ qualitatively from those obtained when a single crop's yield increases. The terms of trade move against agriculture by 9.5 per cent. Again, though real wages decrease by 4.3 per cent, the increase in employment in agriculture is small at 2.2 per cent. If full employment is assumed, the expansion is muted and GDP increases by only 2.6 per cent. As a result, the increase in domestic demand and in non-agricultural supply are smaller, agricultural prices fall further and the terms of trade decrease by 13.6 per cent. Large farmers' real incomes now decrease by 1.5 per cent.

5. Cutting Fertilizer Subsidies

Binswanger and Quizon simulated the effect of subsidising fertilizer prices by 20 per cent. When they conducted their study in the early 1980s, the subsidy was small, between 3 to 6 billion rupees. Since the non-agricultural sector is exogenous in their model, the implicit assumption is that the subsidy is an injection from outside the economy, e.g. foreign aid. The fertilizer subsidy in 1989-90 was about 46 billion rupees and in the base year, 1983-84, the fertilizer subsidy accounted for 16 per cent of total subsidies. Increasing fertilizer subsidies is clearly not an issue at the present time, so I consider instead cutting these subsidies. In addition, since a reduction in the government deficit appears desirable at this juncture, the decrease in fertilizer subsidy is not neutralised by a reduction in taxes or an increase in other expenditure.

I assume that the subsidies on domestic and imported fertilizer are cut by 80 per cent. Since the outcome will depend on the assumed elasticity of capital-labour substitution in fertilizer production, a sensitivity analysis is conducted with respect to this parameter and the labour market closure. Three different values (0.5, 0.8 and 1.1) are used for this parameter and the results for the scenarios with elasticities of 0.8 and 1.1 (Scenarios 5B and 5C) are shown in Table 18. However, the results are not sensitive to this parameter. The after-subsidy price of fertilizer increases by 16.2 per cent when the elasticity is taken to be 0.5, 17.8 per cent when it is 0.8 and 18.9 per cent when it is 1.1. The corresponding decreases in fertilizer output are 10.8 per cent, 12.1 per cent and 13 per cent. The price received by fertilizer producers decreases by 7.2 per cent, 5.8 per cent and 4.8 per cent, respectively. The major impact is on value added and employment in the fertilizer sector, which decline by around 40 per cent.

Fertilizer use decreases by 10.4 per cent in Scenario 5B and 11 per cent in 5C. These decreases are some 28 per cent smaller than those predicted by a partial equilibrium analysis based on the own-price elasticity of -0.84. But the effect on agriculture is small: agricultural value added decreases by 0.3 per cent to 0.4 per cent and GDP decreases by about 0.5 per cent. Crop output is clearly insensitive to fertilizer price, the reason being that the share of fertilizer in total cost is small, about 0.05. The composition of agricultural output and input and labour use change along the lines suggested by the cross-price elasticities in Table 13. The output of rice, wheat and other crops falls while that of coarse cereals increases. Use of animal power, a complement to fertilizer, decreases. Since labour is a substitute for fertilizer, employment in crop agriculture increases (though not total agricultural employment in crop and livestock sectors). Little changes under full employment except that the fall in agricultural value added is smaller, less than 0.1 per cent. This result is at variance with Binswanger and Quizon's finding that a 20 per cent subsidy increases agricultural output by about 1.3 per cent. The difference stems from the fact that their model has an exogenous non-agricultural sector (so that giving a subsidy to fertilizer production does not change non-agricultural value added) and because they assumed the subsidy to be financed by a transfer from the rest of the world[24]. The effect on household incomes is also small; all household groups face small decreases in incomes, the largest being about 1 per cent for urban capitalist households. Comparing the decrease in value added and the decrease in subsidy (for an elasticity of 0.8 for the fertilizer sector), with partial adjustment of wages value added in agriculture decreases by Rs 1.5 billion, value added in fertilizers by Rs 2.6 billion and the fertilizer subsidy by Rs 7.5 billion. Under full employment, these figures become Rs 446 million, Rs 2.6 billion and Rs 7.5 billion. The bulk of the subsidy therefore accrues to the fertilizer sector and not to agriculture[25].

Though the loss in the aggregate to agriculture from a cut in subsidy is relatively small, the loss is very unevenly distributed because of the wide range in fertilizer intensity across the country. The fact that farmers in some parts of the country stand to lose very substantially from the withdrawal of the subsidy could account for the strength of farmers' opposition to such cutbacks. In addition, one cannot rule out the possibility that farmers may not be aware of how much the fertilizer price will rise if the subsidy is withdrawn, i.e. they overestimate the likely increase in price and assume that the price will go up by the same amount as the decrease in subsidy.

6. Food Subsidy Policy

In Scenario 6A, the procurement price is set equal to the open market price, the procurement equation is dropped and procurement is set to zero, as are subsidised sales[26]. At the same time indirect taxes are decreased by the same absolute amount to keep government savings constant[27]. The food subsidy decreases 77 per cent (the cost of storing the buffer stock remains and does not go to zero). All agricultural prices increase: rice by 2.6 per cent, wheat by 0.35 per cent, coarse cereals by 0.74 per cent and other crops by 0.39 per cent. Rice prices go up more than do wheat prices because in the base year the procurement price for rice is only 70 per cent of market price while that for wheat is 90 per cent of market price. Only rice output increases. Agricultural incomes increase, but the increase in food prices results in somewhat lower real incomes for the landless and small farmers, while medium and large farmers make gains. Of course, urban worker and marginal households, the erstwhile recipients of the food subsidy, lose[28]. The losses to urban worker and marginal households are Rs 2.5 billion each, while the food subsidy falls by Rs 9.3 billion. Part of this decrease in the subsidy is accounted for by the decrease in purchase of trade and transport margins by the food subsidy programme. Some of the expenditure on trade and transport margins is transferred as value added to workers and owners of enterprises in the service sector, which is why doing away with the food subsidy programme results in decreases in real incomes for the landless and small farmers also.

In Scenario 6B, rice and wheat procurement are increased by 5 per cent and subsidised sales are increased by as much as procurement increases. Government savings are kept constant by increasing indirect taxes (6B1) or by increasing the direct tax rate for large farmers and urban capitalists (6B2)[29]. This requires increasing procurement prices by 14.3 per cent for rice and 7.4 per cent for wheat. The food subsidy increases by 32.5 per cent and the subsidy to consumers 7.6 per cent (7.3 per cent when direct taxes are increased). Rice and wheat prices increase and other agricultural prices decrease. Agricultural value added rises slightly and non-agricultural value added falls, except that value added in services increases because of the demand for trade and transport services associated with the increased procurement and sales. When increased procurement is financed by raising indirect taxes, the non-agricultural sectors contract more than when the financing is through the income tax. When indirect taxes are used for financing all nominal incomes decline, except for the urban marginal households; all real incomes decline as well. When the income tax is used, all nominal incomes increase, except for large farmer and capitalist households, who are assumed to pay for the increase in procurement. However, because of the increase in food prices, real incomes decrease for all but the recipients of subsidised food, the urban worker and marginal households, whose real incomes increase by 0.05 per cent and 0.18 per cent. It is interesting to note that the distortionary losses from higher indirect taxes result in decreases in nominal and real incomes for all household groups, including the recipients of subsidised cereals.

Thus removing the procurement and subsidy programme entirely and enhancing procurement and subsidised sales both generate losses for the beneficiary households when carried out in a way that maintains government savings constant by varying the indirect tax rate uniformly. That abolishing food subsidies and procurement results in losses for beneficiary households suggests that the benefits to the beneficiaries are larger than the losses resulting from distortions. That increasing procurement and subsidised sales also results in losses for these households implies that marginal benefits are smaller than the marginal distortionary losses. Indeed, reducing procurement of wheat and rice by 5 per cent and reducing indirect taxes simultaneously in order to keep government savings constant produces real income gains for all classes. However, if direct taxes are used to finance the increased subsidy, the distortion is smaller and real incomes increase for household groups receiving subsidised food. This suggests that how food subsidies are financed is of crucial importance in determining whether the intended beneficiaries gain from these subsidies. In the absence of non-distortionary financing, an increase in subsidy may well result in a decrease in welfare for all groups in the population, *including* those receiving the increased subsidy.

Increasing procurement requires paying a higher procurement price, which is paid on the entire amount procured. If subsidised sales rise by as much as procurement, the increase in consumer subsidy is proportional to the increase in procurement. In addition, the trade and transport margins on the increased procurement have also to be paid. So the increase in consumer subsidy is smaller (by a factor of 4, as Table 19 shows) than the increase in government expenditure on the subsidy programme, which is financed by increasing indirect taxes. This is another reason why the distortionary losses outweigh the gains from increased subsidy. Clearly, it would be more efficient to decrease the subsidised sale price than to increase the quantity of subsidised sales. For the same increase in consumer subsidy, government expenditure increases much less under the latter scenario because procurement costs increase much less, if at all, and because storage and transport costs do not increase either, since the quantity procured or sold does not increase. Therefore, the increase in indirect taxes (and the associated distortion) required to finance the same increase in consumer subsidy will be smaller in this scenario and the marginal benefit larger.

Scenario 6B3 illustrates this point. Here the subsidised sale price is reduced to provide the same increase in consumer subsidy as in Scenario 6B1 and this increase is paid for by increasing indirect taxes. Total food subsidies increase by only 3.78 per cent, i.e. 11.6 per cent of the increase in the food subsidy bill in Scenarios 6B1 and 6B2. Rural real incomes decline by 0.016 per cent, urban workers gain 0.012 per cent, urban marginal households gain 0.067 per cent and capitalists lose 0.036 per cent, which is superior to the outcome in Scenario 6B1, where increased procurement was funded by increased indirect taxes. Comparing the outcomes in Scenarios 6B1 and 6B3 one finds that for the same increase in total food subsidy, decreasing the sale price of subsidised food gives a substantially larger increase in the incomes of the beneficiaries than does increased procurement funded by income taxation. However, it also results in larger losses for rural classes other than large farmers. When the food subsidy is increased by increasing procurement and subsidised sales, rural landless and small farmer households stand to gain more than when the subsidy is increased by decreasing the subsidised sale price, even though they do not receive any subsidised food items, because increased procurement and subsidised sales quantities means increased expenditure on the trade sector, some of which flows as wages or profits to the landless and small farmers.

In Scenario 7, the food subsidy is allocated to urban marginal and rural landless and small farmer households in proportion to their population[30]. The reallocation of income to households which spend more on cereals has the effect of raising food prices slightly. The landless and small farmers gain 1.6 per cent and 1.8 per cent, quite sizable gains when compared, for example, to the gains from a 10 per cent yield increase for wheat in Scenario 1C. Urban worker and marginal households lose because under the new allocation the former receive no subsidies and the latter a smaller part of the subsidy. While the gains to the rural poor are significant, it must be borne in mind that the incremental cost-benefit ratio for the procurement and food subsidy system is high.

7. Summary of Results

Several major themes emerge from these scenarios. The liberalisation scenarios confirm the hypothesis of Krueger *et al.* that restrictions and tariffs on agricultural trade represent only a small burden on agriculture and that the main source of taxation of agriculture is the protection provided to the non-agricultural sectors. Direct effects on agriculture are small and general equilibrium effects are important. Thus liberalisation of trade in unprocessed commodities produces only a small change in agricultural value added — a small increase in the medium run, when wages move with the price of food and a small decrease when wages rise and full employment is reached in the long run — and a much larger increase in non-agricultural value added through linkages to agro-processing sectors. The urban classes gain most from liberalisation. When liberalisation is extended to processed commodities, such as edible oils, sugar and processed food, the impact on agriculture is adverse because the decrease in derived demand from these sectors outweighs the positive influence of liberalisation on rice and wheat prices. However, because of non-agricultural expansion and lower food prices, real incomes increase for all groups, though in the long run, these gains are smaller and become negligible for large farmers.

When non-agricultural trade is also liberalised, the major impact on agriculture is through the 26 per cent devaluation required to maintain external balance, which results in substantially higher prices for rice and wheat, but has little effect on prices of coarse cereals (trade in which is insignificant) and other crops, where the effects of devaluation and liberalisation of imports work in opposite directions. While complete liberalisation has the desired effect of raising agricultural income and the nominal incomes of all rural classes, the accompanying increase in food prices negates these gains for all but large farmers in the medium run, and large and medium farmers in the long run. As expected, all urban incomes decrease. These results can be interpreted as suggesting that before the growth-enhancing effects of liberalisation set in, working through capital accumulation and reallocation of resources, trade liberalisation provides no gains in real incomes and has an adverse impact on the rural and urban poor. For liberalisation to be sustainable may require aid to the poor until such time as growth resumes, but this is a topic outside the purview of this study.

Higher world food prices have little impact if India's trade is not liberalised, which is not surprising given the small trade shares before liberalisation. When India's agricultural trade is liberalised, the increase in GDP is smaller with higher world agricultural prices in the medium run because of the link between food prices and wages. In the long run, with full employment, this link is absent and, as would be expected for a net exporter of agricultural commodities, higher world agricultural prices result in higher GDP. However, though higher world prices result in higher incomes for the rural classes, the increase in food prices overwhelms the increase in income for the landless and small farmers, whose real incomes therefore fall. When liberalisation in India is extended to trade in non-agricultural products and higher world food prices coincide with a large devaluation, the effects on distribution are even more pronounced. Though higher world food prices reverse the decrease in GDP seen even in the long run when there is complete trade liberalisation, the gains are restricted to medium and large farmers and all other groups' real incomes fall. In the context of trade liberalisation, higher world food prices only exacerbate the problem of how to safeguard the poor in the interim before liberalisation produces higher growth.

The scenarios on technical change confirm the thesis that the poor, both rural and urban, stand to gain from productivity growth in agriculture with flexible prices and that the distribution of gains from increased productivity is critically dependent on the degree to which prices change, which in turn depends on the degree of openness of the economy. Thus in an economy with state trading in agriculture, if agricultural trade is kept constant, the terms of trade move against agriculture and nominal incomes in agriculture decrease. However, because of the large decline in agricultural prices and large weight that food items have in the budgets of the poor, the landless and small farmers gain. On the other hand, nominal incomes in non-agriculture increase because of the change in terms of trade and the urban classes gain both from the increase in non-agricultural incomes and the fall in food prices. Medium farmers make small gains and large farmers either make small gains or losses. The losses for agriculture are smaller in the medium run because the fall in food prices results in lower wages and therefore stimulates expansion. In the long run, under full employment, wages are higher and employment lower, the non-agricultural expansion smaller and the terms of trade move further against agriculture, producing higher losses for large farmers. Such losses for farm households can be a serious concern because of the possibility of lower farm savings and investment, which in the long run can result in slower productivity growth. Hence there is a need to maintain incentives for large farm households. With trade the movement of the terms of trade against agriculture is moderated. As the level of trade increases, the distribution of gains moves increasingly in favour of rural households and within these in favour of the large farmers. Trade policy, this suggests, is a key factor in determining the distribution of productivity gains and in maintaining incentives for agriculture. In a closed economy, productivity gains in agriculture, a flex-price sector, are transferred to the other sectors and are not retained by the agricultural sector. Trade furnishes a means of moderating this transfer out of agriculture. Government procurement can also perform this function, but as the rough comparison above shows, it is better to support agricultural incomes by exporting rice than by buying rice and supplying it at a subsidised price to urban consumers because the gains to rural and urban households are by and large higher under the former policy than under the latter.

The fertilizer subsidy simulation reconfirms in a general equilibrium framework the finding that the subsidy is largely a subsidy to the fertilizer sector, not to agriculture. The major point to emerge from this exercise is that much of the transfer to agriculture "leaks out" to other sectors and that the subsidy does little to enhance farm output or income.

The food subsidy scenarios demonstrate that how the food subsidy is financed is crucial in determining the outcome. At the margin, the distortionary costs of higher indirect taxes are larger than the benefits from an increase in procurement and sales of rice and wheat and even the household classes receiving the increased subsidy fail to benefit from it. On the other hand, the same increase in subsidy, if financed by an increase in income tax, produces substantial benefits for the recipient classes. Furthermore, holding subsidised sales prices constant, an increase in consumer subsidy brought about by increased procurement and sales requires about nine times the outlay that is required for the same increase in consumer subsidy brought about by lowering subsidised sale prices while keeping sale quantities constant. If indirect taxation is to be used to finance the subsidy, clearly the distortionary losses for a given increase in consumer subsidy will be substantially larger for the first scheme than for the second.

Notes and References

1. For brevity's sake this variant is not used for other scenarios and, in addition, for most scenarios, results are tabulated only for the case where the wage adjusts partially to the price of food.

2. Of course, in a dynamic model of the economy expansion based on foreign borrowing does have a cost because of the repayments required at a later date.

3. Again, because of the focus on the medium term, the model abstracts from accumulation and growth, hence the effects of investment on capital stocks and on productivity growth are excluded.

4. This is a topic of much current interest because of recent moves by the new government in India to drop restrictions on agricultural exports. It is too soon to draw any conclusion about the results of these changes in policy.

5. Exceptions to this are rural small-scale enterprises and sugar factories. But sugar producers in many Indian states have strong links with political parties and are not without influence.

6. For example, in recent years the government has had to stockpile groundnut oil in order to prop up groundnut prices.

7. Of course, this will also mean that non-agricultural trade liberalisation will face even greater opposition than liberalisation which is restricted to agriculture and agricultural processing sectors.

8. Recent moves to reduce the fertilizer subsidy aroused such opposition that the government had to retreat and declare that part of the cut would be reinstated for small and medium farmers.

9. So large is the variation that Faridkot district of Punjab and West Godavari district of Andhra Pradesh consume as much fertilizer as the states of Assam and Orissa combined. (Gulati and Sharma, 1991).

10. Unlike in a macro model, to a first approximation, reducing government spending does not have a contractionary effect because of the neo-classical closure employed: a decrease in the government deficit produces a corresponding increase in private investment.

11. All indirect taxes are increased by the same amount to raise the required amount of revenue. Taxes on unprocessed agricultural products are zero to start with and remain at zero.

12. The expansion in some sectors is the result of the aggregation involved in other crops. Liberalisation of trade in other crops, for example, should not directly affect the sugar sector because sugar cane is a non-tradable. However, lacking an econometrically

estimated supply model which disaggregates other crops further, little improvement in modelling can be expected.

13. Any prediction about sugar exports must be viewed with caution because the world sugar market is far from being competitive.

14. However, the fertilizer import subsidy is retained because the devaluation required to maintain external balance is large and removing the subsidy on top of this devaluation would increase the fertilizer price substantially and produce an improbably large increase in domestic fertilizer production.

15. With full employment, this changes slightly to 27.3 per cent. This should be compared with the 25 per cent over-valuation assumed by Gulati *et al.* (1990a) in their discussion of nominal and effective rates of protection for agriculture.

16. The price increases (from a RUNS projection) are 23 per cent for rice, 15 per cent for wheat, 19.7 per cent for coarse cereals, 22.3 per cent for sugar, 23.2 per cent for oil and 20 per cent for other foods and other crops.

17. Neutral technical change enters the profit function as a factor multiplying prices. Its effect on output supply and factor demands is found by multiplying crop prices in the supply and demand equations by the technical change parameter and by multiplying the supply equation by the technical change parameter for the crop in question. It should be noted that Binswanger and Quizon considered a 20 per cent yield increase. I consider a 10 per cent increase because a 20 per cent increase would produce extremely large changes in prices. Since their model was a linearised one, the effect of a 10 per cent increase in their model would be exactly half of that with a 20 per cent yield increase.

18. Notice that the export quota for rice was specified not in absolute terms, but by specifying that the actual export-domestic sales ratio would be a fixed proportion of the desired ratio (see Chapter 2, Section 2.5). This does not preclude using an absolute quota, as is done in Scenario 4B.

19. Since the general price index is the numéraire, all prices and wages are real prices and wages and the distinction between wages and real wages or prices and real prices will not be maintained in the rest of this study.

20. Using a time-series model, Rangarajan (1982) found that a 1 per cent increase in agricultural output in 1963 (about 0.5 per cent of GDP) gave rise to a short-run increase of 0.5 per cent and a long-run increase of 0.76 per cent in GDP, implying a multiplier of between 1 and 1.25. One might expect the multiplier to have increased since then because production and consumption linkages between agriculture and the rest of the economy have gained in strength over the intervening years. One linkage that is of importance in the CGE model is that between food prices and real non-agricultural wages. As food prices go down, so do real wages, causing non-agricultural employment and output to increase.

21. Both models assume full employment with a agricultural labour supply elasticity with respect to the real wage of 0.3. They found labour demand to increase by 1.1 per cent for a 20 per cent yield increase, i.e. 0.55 per cent for a 10 per cent yield increase. As they point out, yield increases may lead to only modest increases in employment because labour requirements per unit output can decrease, a finding that is confirmed here.

22. The outcomes under full employment are not reported.

23. The marketed surplus for coarse cereals is a small fraction of production (around 10 to 12 per cent for sorghum), so that external trade will likely remain unimportant for some time.

24. Another difference is that Binswanger and Quizon assume a supply elasticity of 4 for fertilizer. Moreover, in the model presented here what matters for fertilizer supply is value added price, not price of output. An increase in output price need not give rise to a

proportionate increase in value added price. In any case, even with a supply elasticity of 4, value added in fertilizer falls 28.8 per cent and value added in agriculture falls 0.12 per cent when the subsidy is cut.

25. Gulati and Sharma (1991) suggest that about half the budgetary subsidy on fertilizers goes to the farmer. They take the per-unit subsidy to be the difference between the cost of imported fertilizer and the price actually paid by the farmer. This is an overestimate because it does not take into account the non-zero demand and supply elasticities for fertilizer.

26. Since procurement and sales are not equal, some change in public stocks takes place. It should be emphasized that since the procurement equations are local approximations to the true relation between procurement, prices and output, simulation results for large changes, such as the elimination of procurement, are likely to be quite inaccurate.

27. The government deficit is not allowed to decrease as the subsidy bill decreases and is kept constant in order to maintain comparability with the other food subsidy scenarios, in which government savings are kept constant.

28. These outcomes are under full employment, they differ insignificantly from those with wages adjusting partially to food prices.

29. Only the full employment simulations are presented here. There is no tax on agricultural income, tax evasion by urban households is common and the share of income tax in total taxes has been declining for several years. So the feasibility of raising the income tax is questionable.

30. Government savings are not kept fixed here because there is no change to the first order in government expenditure or revenue.

Chapter 4

Conclusion

The major policy issues facing Indian agriculture today stem from the style of growth India has followed for several decades. Agricultural growth has been dependent on two crops, rice and wheat. New technology for these crops became available in the mid-1960s and proved to be easily adaptable to local conditions. The lack of a similarly successful land-saving technology for other crops has meant that regions unsuited for intensive rice or wheat cultivation for agroclimatic or institutional reasons have tended to lag behind regions where the Green Revolution technology has proved successful. Large differences have come to exist across regions in growth rates of yield and output and levels of income and poverty. Large-scale rural poverty is concentrated in regions of poor agricultural performance. Reducing poverty in these regions remains a major task.

Government intervention in agriculture has been pervasive for several reasons. Intervention in the economy was legitimised by the early adherence to economic planning. The exigencies of feeding urban areas in an era of chronic food shortages led to the development of a large-scale food subsidy programme and control over foreign trade. Later, the need to foster adoption of new technology was seen as requiring subsidies for new inputs and, at a later stage, government price supports for rice and wheat, the major crops to benefit from the new technology. The price support and procurement interventions also made possible the continuation of the food subsidy programme without the need to resort to imports.

A complex and changing structure of incentives and disincentives has emerged from these interventions. The early tendency to tax rice and wheat producers by maintaining prices at or below cost of production has given way to procurement prices that are well above the cost of production in most years in areas producing a large marketed surplus. In other areas, where the marketed surplus and government purchases are small, the farm harvest price is above cost of production and procurement is ineffective. The data on nominal and effective protection coefficients suggest that rice is taxed and the price of wheat is in the range where autarky is a possibility. Data on other crops suggest that most are protected, except cotton, and that the NPCs/EPCs have been increasing over time. Input subsidies have increased rapidly because governments have been unable or unwilling to push through price increases as costs have increased, e.g. of fertilizer after the oil shock. Agroclimatic, infrastructural

63

and institutional differences between regions have resulted in large differences in nominal and effective protection coefficients for the same crop and in the regions' shares of agricultural subsidies. These interventions have major implications at the regional level, for cropping patterns, resource allocation, efficiency and income distribution. But the net effect of these interventions, most observers note, is small for the agricultural sector as a whole. As a result, some of the greatest impacts of measures to liberalise agricultural trade or to reduce agricultural subsidies or other interventions in agriculture will be felt at the regional level. Agricultural liberalisation will also affect the non-agricultural sector directly because several agricultural interventions, such as agricultural subsidies and the food procurement and subsidy programme, have a direct impact on the non-agricultural sector. In addition, given the importance of agriculture as a producer of tradables and the importance of agricultural products in the household budget, changes in the volume and composition of agricultural output resulting from liberalisation will also have important repercussions on the non-agricultural sector.

Two key issues emerge here. Firstly, how will agricultural and industrial liberalisation in India affect the agricultural sector and the rest of the economy and what are the consequences for output and trade and for the distribution of income in the urban and rural sectors? Secondly, under different domestic liberalisation scenarios, what will be the impact of higher world prices resulting from agricultural trade liberalisation by the OECD countries on the agricultural and non-agricultural sectors, and on different economic classes?

Several conclusions may be drawn from the domestic liberalisation scenarios. Firstly, the net effect of direct interventions in agriculture is small, so that the major impact of liberalising India's agricultural trade is on the non-agricultural sector and not on agriculture itself. Secondly, liberalisation of trade in processed agricultural commodities has an adverse impact on agriculture because of the high level of protection on these commodities. Thirdly, the impact of industrial liberalisation on agriculture is much larger than that of agricultural liberalisation. However, while liberalisation of industrial trade stimulates agricultural expansion by raising agricultural prices, it also produces losses in real incomes for all but the large farmers. Lastly, there are substantial differences between the medium-run and long-run outcomes. In the medium run, wages are sensitive to food prices, so that when food prices increase, wages increase as well. In the long run, wages are determined by market clearing. In scenarios in which agriculture expands in response to higher prices, wages are higher in the long run than in the medium run. Hence output is lower in the long run. Similarly, industrial expansion and contraction are weaker in the long run. Thus GDP growth is lower in the long run than in the medium run. In scenarios in which the terms of trade move in favour of agriculture, agricultural wages are lower and non-agricultural wages higher in the medium run than under full employment. Thus, in the long run, in these scenarios, the increase in agricultural output is smaller and agricultural prices higher than in the short run. As the labour market adjusts in the long run, non-agricultural wages fall in these scenarios and the non-agricultural sector shrinks less than in the medium run, so that non-agricultural output is larger and prices lower. The improvement in the terms of trade for agriculture is therefore larger in the long run. Hence the distribution of income in the long run differs markedly from that in the medium run, with higher food prices tilting the distribution in favour of medium and large farmers.

The effect of higher world agricultural prices on India is negligible if India's trade is not liberalised because trade shares in agriculture are small initially, so that the degree of price transmission is also small. When higher world agricultural prices and liberalisation of India's agricultural trade coincide, price transmission is larger and this proves to be contractive in the medium run, while being expansionary in the long run. In both the medium and long run, higher world food prices lead to losses in real income for all but the medium and large farmers. These effects are exacerbated when liberalisation extends to non-agriculture, resulting in a removal of the indirect disprotection of agriculture and a large change in the terms of trade in favour of agriculture. Higher world agricultural prices push the terms of trade further in this direction, resulting in larger increases in agricultural value added, and larger decreases in real incomes for the rural poor and all urban classes.

\ These results suggest that liberalisation, especially economy-wide liberalisation, while enhancing efficiency and output in the long run, has the potential for creating large changes in income distribution and decreasing the real incomes of all but medium and large farmers in the medium and long run, before increases in productivity resulting from resource reallocation and investment begin to make themselves felt. Higher world agricultural prices will only serve to accentuate these changes.

Agricultural growth, as the scenarios of yield increases demonstrate, remains an effective means of poverty alleviation, despite the fact that agricultural labour demand is not highly responsive to growth, so long as agricultural prices are allowed to fall, permitting the transfer of some of the gains from growth to consumers. In the absence of trade liberalisation, the fall in prices is so great that real incomes fall for large farmers. But to sustain agricultural growth requires maintaining incentives for continued investment. Trade can be used to support agricultural prices and ensure that productivity gains in agriculture flow out to net buyers of food while maintaining positive incentives for producer households.

The fertilizer subsidy and food subsidy scenarios demonstrate that these interventions have substantial impacts on the non-agricultural sector. The fertilizer subsidy has little effect on farm incomes and output. In the case of the food subsidy, the major finding is that the net benefits at the margin are very sensitive to how the subsidy is financed. If the subsidy is financed by raising indirect taxes, the distortionary costs of the higher tax outweigh the gains from the subsidy even for the recipients of the subsidy. However, when the subsidy is paid for by raising income taxes, the net benefits are strongly positive for recipients.

Building a SAM for India

The SAM developed for this study is essentially an updated and disaggregated version of that built by Subbarao and de Janvry (1986) around the 1977-78 input-output table for India. The SAM used here is based on the 115-sector 1983-84 input-output table. The procedure used in building the SAM was as follows. The input-output table and its associated subsidy and tax vectors form the core of the SAM. To obtain a SAM from this core, value added in each sector has to be disaggregated into payments to various factors and these factor payments have to be distributed to the institutions in the SAM. In addition, the institutional accounts, which are present in rudimentary form in the input-output table, have to be disaggregated and made complete. The first step, then, is to disaggregate and distribute factor incomes. Following this, the institutional accounts are disaggregated.

The make matrix in the input-output table presented some difficulty because in it the agricultural activities supply some non-agricultural commodities and vice versa. Because this would complicate the modelling unnecessarily and because the changes involved were small, the make matrix was block-diagonalised, so that crop agriculture did not produce any non-agricultural commodity and vice versa. The changes involved are small since the fraction of agricultural output that is accounted for by non-agricultural commodities is small, less than 0.3 per cent except for one entry which is 1.3 per cent. The fraction of non-agricultural output which is accounted for by agricultural commodities is nowhere larger than 0.75 per cent.

1. Disaggregating Factor Incomes

In building their SAM, Subbarao and de Janvry divided agricultural valued added into payments to hired and family labour and gross profits, using data from studies of cost of cultivation in the late 1960s and early 1970s. These were then allocated to different land-holding classes following a study by Ali *et al.*, taking into account differences in cropping pattern across farms of different size classes and differences in labour availability across the different land-holding classes. In this manner, both the generation and distribution of agricultural value added were determined. In the case of the livestock sector, Ali *et al.* used livestock census data to allocate valued added from livestock to the rural household groups.

Since the share of labour in agricultural costs has declined significantly since the 1970s, this exercise was repeated using more recent data on costs of cultivation and labour absorption for several crops (reported in Gulati *et al.*, 1990, and Gulati and Sharma, 1990c). For want of better information, value added in livestock was divided into wages and gross profits using the same ratio as in agriculture and it was assumed that only family labour is used in the livestock sector, so that both wages and profits flow to households in the same proportion[1].

Non-agricultural value added was disaggregated into income of the self-employed, wages and profits using the shares reported at a highly aggregated level in the national accounts (CSO, 1987). As noted above in Chapter 2, Section 2.1, it is assumed that the informal sector provides income only to the self-employed so that valued added in the informal sector is the same as the income of the self-employed. The weakness of the data on the informal sector necessitates this simplification[2]. The share of the self-employed in sectors such as fertilizers, public administration and intermediates was assumed to be zero, as was the share of profits in public administration. Unlike agricultural income, which is assumed to flow only to rural households, non-agricultural incomes flow to both rural and urban households. However, as noted in Chapter 2, Section 1 above, rural landless non-agricultural households receive no agricultural income and are considered part of the urban sector. Non-agricultural factor incomes are distributed to the urban and rural classes as follows. Capitalists receive only non-agricultural profits and workers only non-agricultural wages. The urban self-employed receive both non-agricultural wages and non-agricultural profits and large farmers do not receive non-agricultural wage income. The shares of the different classes in non-agricultural incomes are based on data from a household income survey conducted in 1976 (National Council of Applied Economic Research, 1980).

2. Institutional Accounts

The institutional accounts are disaggregated in several steps. The first step is to obtain an aggregated SAM with a single account for all households. This requires a knowledge of private consumption at producer price and at market price and of transactions between institutions, i.e., between households, government, the capital account, the stock change account and the rest of the world. These latter are obtained from national accounts data on taxes, transfers to households, remittances and savings. Little information is available on the incidence across household groups of taxes and transfers. Direct taxes are paid predominantly by urban classes, the capitalists and workers. Remittances from the rest of the world were allocated uniformly to all groups. The food subsidy was assumed, as noted above, to accrue only to the urban workers and self-employed, in proportion to their population.

The next step is to obtain consumption at producer price and at market price. These have to be built up using the flows at factor cost in the 115-sector 1983-84 input-output table and data on taxes, subsidies and transport margins provided with the table. Taxes on commodities are divided into import and export duties, excise, sales tax and other taxes. However, for subsidies similar information is not provided and only a vector of subsidy by commodity is available. Unfortunately, the allocation of subsidies is problematic. The subsidy shown for food commodities, for example, consists of subsidies for irrigation, the so-called consumer subsidy on subsidised commodities and export subsidies. Of course, a large part of this consumer subsidy is really just purchases of trade and transport services because the consumer subsidy as defined by the government includes the costs of buffer stock storage. The subsidies were allocated to food subsidies (i.e. the true consumer subsidy plus purchases of trade and transport services), irrigation subsidies (using the value added from irrigation reported in the national accounts), export subsidies (using the incomplete information to be found in budget documents), and other subsidies (amongst them the subsidy to fertilizer). Part of the total fertilizer subsidy is on imported fertilizer, but the figure reported for the subsidy on imported fertilizer also includes the costs of carrying fertilizer stocks and is too large compared to the CIF value of fertilizer imports, so the subsidy rate on imported and domestic fertilizer was assumed to be the same.

Not all uses of a commodity are subsidised or taxed to the same extent. However, lacking data on the incidence by use, it was assumed that the incidence was uniform across all uses (except that the export subsidy applied only to exports). On this basis, the matrices of import duties, subsidies and other indirect taxes paid by activities and institutions were obtained by allocating subsidies and taxes proportionately to all uses[3]. While these matrices give the correct tax and subsidy by commodity, they do not yield the correct net indirect taxes paid by each activity and institution because the incidence of taxes and subsidies is not uniform across uses as assumed. The RAS procedure (Dervis, *et al.*) was used to adjust these matrices to obtain the correct net taxes paid by use and by commodity. Adding these matrices to the flows at factor cost gives flows at producer price. These flows at producer price were then converted to flows at market price using trade and transport margins reported in the *Technical Note on the Sixth Plan* (1985) and then aggregated to the 17-sector level.

3. Household Consumption

The only data available on savings rates for different expenditure or income class are those from the survey referred to above. These savings rates were also used by de Janvry and Subbarao for their SAM. These savings rates were adjusted proportionately in order to obtain the observed aggregate private savings in the national accounts for 1983. Based on these savings rates and the household incomes obtained above, estimates of expenditure were obtained for each household group. Using budget shares from the National Sample Survey on consumption for 1983-84 at the expenditure levels obtained in the SAM, a matrix of consumption demand at market price was obtained for the seven household groups for the 14 commodities covered by the National Sample Survey (i.e. the 17 commodities in the SAM, with the exception of fertilizer, animal services and public administration). The RAS procedure was used to adjust this matrix so as to agree with the aggregate consumption vector obtained earlier. The adjusted matrix was converted back to producer prices and used in the SAM.

69

Notes and References

1. These sectors are not as important as the crop-producing sectors and so this cursory treatment of factor incomes should not be a fatal defect. In the input-output table, the draft animal services sector sells its output to agriculture at cost. I correct this by assuming a 25 per cent value added-to-output ratio and increasing the value of sales to agriculture, decreasing agricultural value added and increasing value added in the draft animal sector accordingly.

2. The methodology for India's national accounts is currently being revised. It is hoped that new data from recent surveys on the informal sector will appear in the national accounts, which would then permit a more sensible disaggregation of the informal sector.

3. In going from flows at factor cost to flows at market price, one reverses the procedure used to obtain the input-output table at factor cost from the basic data on flows at market prices. This procedure requires knowing the allocation of subsidies and taxes by use. Unfortunately, the Central Statistical Organisation presents only the vector of subsidies and taxes and not the matrix of taxes and subsidies underlying their computations.

The Model

The equations of the model are displayed in Appendix 3. This is a standard CGE model but for two features: the use of a multi-market specification for agriculture and the labour market closure. The first eight equations define the different sets of prices in the model. Equation 1 defines the price producers receive for exports, PE_i, in terms of the world price, the exchange rate and price wedges created by taxes, subsidies and transport margins. Equation 2 states that the market price is the producer price plus trade and transport margins. The third equation defines the value of absorption as the sum of domestic sales inclusive of taxes and subsidies, imports inclusive of tariffs, and in the case of rice and wheat, subsidised sales (valued at procurement price). Equation 4 (for commodities other than rice and wheat) states that the value of total output equals the value of domestic sales and changes in stocks (valued at the domestic sale price) and exports valued at the export price. The fifth equation relates commodity prices (P_i^s) to activity prices (P_i^a) for the non-agricultural sectors using coefficients from the make matrix. The sixth equation states that the price of value added in the non-agricultural sectors is the activity price less intermediate costs per unit of output. The seventh equation defines the aggregate price index, the numéraire in the model, and the eighth the food price indices for agricultural and non-agricultural workers.

The next block of equations are for the procurement and food subsidy system, and apply only to rice and wheat. Equation 9 states that total output (X_i^s) equals open-market sales (Q_i^{om}) plus procurement (Q_i^{pr}). Equation 10 is an econometrically estimated relation (Gulati and Sharma, 1990a), which states that the quantity procured is a linear function of production and the ratio between procurement and open market prices. Equation 11 defines total change in stocks to equal changes in private stocks (ΔS_i^p) plus the change in government stocks, which is the difference between the quantity procured and the quantity sold. Equation 12 defines the value of total output to equal the value of open market sales and procurement. Equation 13 defines the value of open market sales as the sum of values of domestic sales, private stock changes and exports. Equations 14 to 17 define various elements of cost. Equation 14 states that the cost of storage is proportional to the amount stored. The cost of running the procurement programme (C^{fd}) is the difference between procurement price plus procurement and distribution costs and the subsidised price times the quantity sold. This cost and the storage cost (together known as the food subsidy) are borne by government. The true consumer subsidy is defined in equation 16, and is the difference between market price and subsidised price times the quantity sold[1]. C^{tr}, the difference between the programme cost (C^{fd}) and the consumer subsidy (C^{con}) is treated as purchase of trade and transport services by the government.

Equations 18 to 22 are for the non-agricultural sectors. Output in the formal sector (Y_j^F) is a CES function of a labour aggregate (L_j^a) and (fixed) sectoral capital stock (K_j). Formal sector output is a fixed fraction of total output (equation 19). Activity output levels are related to commodity outputs through the make matrix coefficients (equation 20), the counterpart of equation 5 for activity and commodity prices. The labour aggregate (L_j^a) employed in sector j is a Cobb-Douglas aggregate of each type of labour demanded (equation 21). Equation 22 is the first-order condition for profit maximisation with respect to employment of each type of labour.

Equations 23 to 26 represent the agricultural supply module, which is based on the generalised quadratic profit function. In these equations the index p runs over the four crops, agricultural labour and draught animal services and v_p is a vector of prices for these items, i.e. producer prices for crops, the wage rate for agricultural labour and the market price of draught animal services. The equations for input demands have a negative sign prefixed as is the convention for the generalised quadratic profit function. Z_b and Z_{fert} are the intermediate demands from agriculture for draught animal services and fertilizer, respectively. The factor α_p is for modelling neutral technical change (or yield increases) and is unity for all inputs and can exceed one only for the crop outputs.

Aggregate labour demand for each type of labour is defined by equation 27. Equations 28 and 29 are two possible market closures: in the first one labour demand equals labour supply and labour supply responds to the real wage with a constant elasticity and in the other, the wage for each type of labour adjusts partially (with a constant elasticity) to changes in the food price index for that labour type. These two closures are to be interpreted as capturing essential features of medium- and long-run labour market behaviour, which determine in some respects the medium- and long-run outcomes of policy reforms. In the medium run, wages are "sticky" and do not respond to labour market pressures; instead they are sensitive to food prices and adjust partially to changes in food prices (Ahluwalia, 1985)[2]. For example, an increase in food prices relative to other prices will push up the wage rate (relative to the numeraire) and since the numeraire is the price index, the real wage rate. In the long run, wages are responsive to market pressures and are determined by full employment.

Equations 30 to 34 model foreign trade. For commodities other than rice and wheat, domestic production is a CET aggregate of domestic sales plus additions to stocks and exports (equation 30). In the case of rice and wheat, the choice of exporting or selling at home applies only to that part of output which reaches the open market (equation 31). The actual ratio of exports to domestic sales plus additions to stocks is a fraction, k_i^x, of the desired ratio, which is obtained by maximising revenues. If k_i^x were unity, there would be no restrictions on exports. Similarly, domestic absorption (X_i) (less subsidised sales in the case of rice and wheat) is a CES aggregate of imports and domestic sales. As for exports, equation 34 states that the actual ratio of imports to domestic sales is a fraction, k_i^m, of the desired ratio, which is a function of the relevant prices. If k^x or k^m is fixed at unity, no restrictions on trade exist. If the quantity of trade is fixed and the corresponding k becomes a free variable, a fixed quota results.

Equations 35 to 37 are for the consumer demand system. Demand is a function of market prices (P_i^m) and disposable income less savings ($y_h^d (1 - mps_h)$). The only non-standard feature is that demand for the last four commodities in the system is given by fixed value shares of demand for an aggregate of these four commodities, the reason being that an LES is not available at this level of aggregation. P_h^C is the geometric price index for this four-commodity aggregate.

Factor incomes are defined in equations 38 to 41. In equation 38, the income of the self-employed is found by adding up a fixed fraction of value added in each non-agricultural sector. Equation 39 defines capital incomes in each non-agricultural sector as value added in the formal sector less payments to labour. Gross profits in agriculture are obtained in equation 40 by subtracting value of inputs and payments to labour from value of crops and adding the irrigation subsidy (assumed to be fixed in real terms). Gross profits in each sector are allocated to agricultural and non-agricultural profits in fixed proportions in equation 41.

Each household class receives fixed shares of wage income, profits, income from self-employment and the consumer subsidy on food, transfers from government, and transfers from the rest of the world (equation 42). Disposable income (y_h^d) is given by income less direct taxes and remittances to the rest of the world (equation 43). Total household taxes and savings are defined in equations 44 and 45. Equation 46 defines government revenues as the sum of indirect and direct taxes plus its share of gross profits. Government savings emerges as a residual in equation 47. Total indirect taxes are obtained in equation 48 and total budgetary subsidies in equation 49. Government consumption demand and investment demand are allocated using fixed shares in equations 50 and 51. Equation 52 defines total savings to be the sum of domestic and foreign savings. Investment is assumed to be equal to savings, which is known as the neo-classical closure. Equations 53 and 54 are the market-clearing conditions[3]. Equation 56 defines the exchange rate regime and equation 57 the current account balance. Since this is a one-period model with no dynamics, foreign borrowing is held constant in the simulations to prevent costless expansion based on increasing external imbalance. Lastly, equation 58 is used to check whether the solution satisfies Walras' law.

The initialisation of the model is straightforward enough. Except for the econometrically estimated parameters of the procurement equation, the demand system and the agricultural supply module, all other parameters are obtained from the SAM or are informed guesses. The tax and subsidy rates were found in the course of building the SAM. The weights for price indices are also computed from data in the SAM. The parameters of the procurement equation are from Gulati and Sharma (1990a) and of the procurement and storage cost equations from Gulati and Sharma (1991). The share of the informal sector, the weights used in obtaining the labour aggregate, the shares of each household class in labour income, profits and income from self-employment, the sectoral break-up of government consumption and investment, direct tax and household savings rates, the shares of government and the rest of the world in gross profits, all these are obtained from the SAM. The base-year export and import world prices are found by assuming that producer prices (and the exchange rate and wage rates) are one in the base year. The elasticity of substitution in the CES production functions is taken to be 0.8, a medium value. For the trade aggregation functions it is expected that the elasticities will be high (15-20) for commodities that are close to being homogenous, such as wheat and rice, medium (2-3) for commodities such as edible oils, and low (0.5) for highly heterogenous commodities such as intermediates. In addition, import elasticities are higher than export elasticities, the idea being that it is easier to import than to export or imports are more price-responsive than exports.

Notes and References

1. The market price used here is not the same as the market price used in the rest of the model. The trade and transport mark-up used here is higher because it applies only to the marketed portion of wheat and rice output, unlike the trade and transport margin used elsewhere which applies to total output of rice and wheat.

2. This is not the same as Keynesian wage rigidity, which depends on money illusion, because purely real CGE models do not have endogenous price levels or money, hence no nominal wages or nominal wage rigidity.

3. Notice that two different sets of I-O coefficients are used here. One is from the usual commodity by activity input use matrix. The other, used solely for the agricultural sector, is a commodity by commodity input use matrix created from the intermediate input matrix for agricultural crops.

The Equations of the Model

Price System

$$PE_i(1 + te_i - se_i + mr_i) = ERPE_i^w \tag{1}$$

$$P_i^m = P_i(1 + mr_i) \tag{2}$$

$$P_i X_i = P_i^d(1 + t_i - s_i)X_i^d + ERPM_i^w(1 + tm_i - sm_i) + I_R(i)P_i^{pr}Q_i^s \tag{3}$$

$$P_i^s X_i^s = P_i^d X_i^d + P_i^d \Delta S_i + PE_i E_i, \quad i \notin R \tag{4}$$

$$P_i^s = \sum_{j \in N} m_{ji} P_j^a, \quad i \in N \tag{5}$$

$$P_j^a = P_j^{va} + \sum_i a_{ij} P_i, \quad j \in N \tag{6}$$

$$\bar{P} = \sum_i c_i P_i^s \tag{7}$$

$$P_l^{fd} = \sum_i \mu_l^{fd} P_i^m \tag{8}$$

Procurement

$$X_i^s = Q_i^{om} + Q_i^{pr}, \quad i \in R \tag{9}$$

$$Q_i^{pr} = a_{0i} + a_{1i} X_i^s + a_{2i} P_i^{pr}/P_i^{om}, \quad i \in R \tag{10}$$

$$\Delta S_i = \Delta S_i^{p} + Q_i^{pr} - Q_i^{s}, \quad i \in R \tag{11}$$

$$P_i^{s} X_i^{s} = P_i^{om} Q_i^{om} + P_i^{pr} Q_i^{pr}, \quad i \in R \tag{12}$$

$$P_i^{om} Q_i^{om} = P_i^{d} X_i^{d} + P_i^{d} \Delta S_i^{p} + P E_i E_i, \quad i \in R \tag{13}$$

$$C^{st} = \bar{P} \sum_{i \in R} (S_i^{0} + \tfrac{1}{2}(Q_i^{pr} - Q_i^{s})) st_i \tag{14}$$

$$C^{fd} = \sum_{i \in R} (P_i^{pr} + \bar{P} pr_i - P_i^{s}) Q_i^{s} \tag{15}$$

$$C^{con} = \sum_{i \in R} ((1 + p_i) P_i - P_i^{s}) Q_i^{s} \tag{16}$$

$$C^{tr} = C^{fd} - C^{con} \tag{17}$$

Production

$$Y_j^{F} = CES(L_j^{a}, K_j), \quad j \in N \tag{18}$$

$$Y_j = Y_j^{F}/(1 - F_j), \quad j \in N \tag{19}$$

$$Y_j = \sum_{i \in N} m_{ji} X_i^{s}, \quad j \in N \tag{20}$$

$$L_j^{a} = \prod_{l} L_{jl}^{\phi_{jl}}, \quad j \in N \tag{21}$$

$$w_l L_{jl} = P_j^{va} \phi_{jl} L_j^a \partial CES(L_j^a, K_j)/\partial L_j^a, \quad j \in N \tag{22}$$

Agricultural Sector

$$X_i^s = \alpha_i (a_i + \sum_{p \in I} b_{ip} \alpha_p v_p / P_{fert}), \quad i \in A \tag{23}$$

$$-L_{crops,ag} = a_{ag} + \sum_{p \in I} b_{ag,p} \alpha_p v_p / P_{fert} \tag{24}$$

$$-Z_b = a_b + \sum_{p \in I} b_{b,p} \alpha_p v_p / P_{fert} \tag{25}$$

$$-Z_{fert} = a_{fert} - \tfrac{1}{2} \sum_{p,q \in I} b_{pq} \alpha_p \alpha_q v_p v_q / P_{fert}^2 \tag{26}$$

Labour Market

$$L_l = \sum_i L_{il} \tag{27}$$

$$L_l = L_l^0 (w_l/w_l^0)^{v_l} \quad \text{full employment, or} \tag{28}$$

$$w_l = w_l^0 (P_l^{fd}/P_{0l}^{fd})^{\eta_l} \quad \text{partially adjusting wages} \tag{29}$$

Trade

$$X_i^s = CET(X_i^d + \Delta S_i, E_i), \quad i \notin R \tag{30}$$

$$Q_i^{om} = CET(X_i^d + \Delta S_i^p, E_i), \quad i \in R \tag{31}$$

$$E_i/(X_i^d + (1 - I_R(i))\Delta S_i + I_R(i)\Delta S_i^p) = k_i^x ((PE_i/P_i^d)(1 - \gamma_i)/\gamma_i)^{1/\rho_i^T} \tag{32}$$

$$X_i - I_R(i)Q_i^s = CES(M_i, X_i^d) \tag{33}$$

$$M_i/X_i^d = k_i^m((P_i^d(1+t_i-s_i)/(ERPW_i^m(1+tm_i-sm_i))\tau_i/(1-\tau_i))^{-1/\rho_i^u} \tag{34}$$

Final Demand

$$P_i^m CD_i = \sum_h (P_i^m \gamma_{ih} + \beta_{ih}(y_h^d(1-mps_h) - P_h^C \gamma_{Ch} - \sum_{j\in C} P_j^m \gamma_{jh})), \quad i\notin C \tag{35}$$

$$P_i^m CD_i = \sum_h W_{ih}(P_h^C \gamma_{Ch} + \beta_{Ch}(y_h^d(1-mps_h) - P_h^C \gamma_{Ch} - \sum_{j\notin C} P_j^m \gamma_{jh})), \quad i\in C \tag{36}$$

$$P_h^C = \prod_{i\in C} P_i^{m\,W_{ih}} \tag{37}$$

Factor Incomes

$$MINC = \sum_{j\in N} P_j^{va} Y_j F_j \tag{38}$$

$$KVA_j = P_j^{va} Y_j^F - \sum_l w_l L_{jl}, \quad j\in N \tag{39}$$

$$KVA_{crop} = \sum_{i\in A} P_i^s X_i^s - w_{ag} L_{crop,ag} - P_{fert} Z_{fert} - P_b Z_b - \sum_{\substack{j\in W \\ i\in A}} a_{ji} P_j X_i^s + \bar{P} IRSUB \tag{40}$$

$$KINC_k = \sum_j KVA_j \kappa_{kj} \tag{41}$$

Institutions

$$y_h = \sum_l \theta_{hl}^L w_l L_l + \sum_k \theta_{hk}^K KINC_k + \theta_h^M MINC + \omega_h^F C^{con} + \bar{P} T_{Gh} + ER T_{Wh} \tag{42}$$

$$y_h^d = (1-dt_h)y_h - ER T_{hW} \tag{43}$$

$$HTAX = \sum_h dt_h y_h \tag{44}$$

$$HSAV = \sum_h y_h^d mps_h \tag{45}$$

$$GR = INDTAX + HTAX + \sum_k G_k KINC_k \tag{46}$$

$$GR = \bar{P}C_G + GSAV + \bar{P}\sum_h T_{Gh} + TOTSUB \tag{47}$$

$$INDTAX = ER\sum_i tm_i PM_i^w M_i + ER\sum_i te_i PE_i^w E_i + \sum_i t_i P_i^d X_i^d \tag{48}$$

$$TOTSUB = ER\sum_i se_i PE_i^w E_i + \sum_i s_i P_i^d X_i^d + ER\sum_i sm_i PM_i^w M_i \\ + \bar{P}\ IRSUB + C^{st} + C^{fd} \tag{49}$$

$$P_i CG_i = S_i^G \bar{P} C_G \tag{50}$$

$$P_i CI_i = S_i^I \bar{P} INV \tag{51}$$

$$TSAV = HSAV + GSAV + ER FBOR \tag{52}$$

Market Constraints

$$X_i = \sum_{j \in N} a_{ij} Y_j + \sum_{j \in A} a_{ij}^{ag} X_j^s + CD_i + CG_i + CI_i \\ + TDMAR/P_{serv}\ \delta_{i,\,serv}, \quad i \notin W \tag{53}$$

$$X_i = \sum_{j \in N} a_{ij} Y_j + Z_i + CD_i + CG_i + CI_i, \quad i \in W \tag{54}$$

$$TDMAR = \sum_i mr_i PE_i E_i + \sum_i mr_i P_i CD_i \tag{55}$$

$$FBOR = FBOR^0 \quad \text{floating exchange rate or} \tag{56}$$

$$ER = E\bar{R}, \quad \text{fixed exchange rate} \tag{57}$$

$$FBOR = \sum_i PM_i^{\,w} M_i - \sum_i PE_i^{\,w} E_i + \sum_h (T_{hW} - T_{Wh}) + \sum_k \theta_k^R KINC_k / ER \tag{58}$$

Walras' Law

$$CTL = TSAV - \bar{P} INV - \sum_{i \notin R} P_i^{\,d} \Delta S_i - \sum_{i \in R} (P_i^{\,d} \Delta S_i^{\,p} + P_i^{\,pr}(Q_i^{\,pr} - Q_i^{\,s})) \tag{59}$$

Sets & Associated Notation

A Set of crop commodities (rice, wheat, coarse cereals, other crops)

N Set of non-agricultural commodities

I Set of agricultural inputs and outputs (crops, labour, fertilizer, animal power)

W Set of agricultural material inputs (fertilizer, animal power)

R Set of subsidised foods (rice, wheat)

C Set of aggregated commodities in demand (consumer goods, intermediates, durables and services)

$$I_A(i) = \begin{cases} 1 & \text{if } i \in A \\ 0 & \text{otherwise} \end{cases}$$

$$\delta_{i,serv} = \begin{cases} 1 & \text{if } i = services \\ 0 & \text{otherwise} \end{cases}$$

Endogenous Variables

PE_i	Export price in domestic currency
$P_i^{\,d}$	Price of domestic sales
$P_i^{\,s}$	Average price received by producers
P_i	Price of domestic absorption
$P_i^{\,m}$	Price of domestic absorption including transport margins
$P_i^{\,a}$	Activity price
$P_i^{\,va}$	Value-added price
$\bar{P}$	Aggregate price index
$P_l^{\,fd}$	Food price index for labour of type l

X_i^s	Total output of commodity i
X_i^d	Domestic sales of commodity i
E_i	Exports of commodity i
M_i	Imports of commodity i
Q_i^{om}	Open market sales of rice or wheat
P_i^{om}	Open market prices of rice or wheat
Q_i^{pr}	Procurement of rice or wheat
ΔS_i^p	Change in private stocks of rice or wheat
C^{st}	Storage cost for public stocks of rice and wheat
C^{fd}	Food subsidy on rice and wheat
C^{con}	Consumer subsidy on rice and wheat
P_h^C	Price of aggregate of consumption goods in set C
C^{tr}	Subsidy on trade and transport costs of food subsidy programme
Y_j^F	Formal sector output for sector j
Y_j	Total output for sector j
L_j^a	Labour aggregate in sector j
L_{jl}	Demand for labour of type l in sector j
L_l	Total demand for labour of type l
w_l	Wage for labour of type l
v_p	Prices of agricultural inputs and outputs
$v_i = P_i^s, \; i \in A$	Producer prices for crops
$v_{ag} = w_{ag}$	Wages for agricultural labour
$v_b = P_b$	Price of animal services
P_{fert}	Fertilizer price
Z_{fert}	Fertilizer demand in agriculture
Z_b	Demand for animal services in agriculture
CD_i	Consumer demand for commodity i
y_h	Income for household of type h
y_h^d	Disposable income for household of type h
$MINC$	Mixed non-crop income of the self-employed
KVA_j	Profits in sector j
$KINC_k$	Profits to capital of type k
$HTAX$	Direct taxes paid by households
$HSAV$	Household savings
$GSAV$	Government savings
$TSAV$	Total savings
CTL	Total savings less total investment (Walras' law)
GR	Government revenue
$INDTAX$	Total indirect taxes
$TOTSUB$	Total subsidies
INV	Real investment
CG_i	Government demand for commodity i
CI_i	Investment demand for commodity i
$TDMAR$	Trade and transport margins
ER	Exchange rate

Policy Variables

P_i^{pr}	Procurement price for rice or wheat
P_i^{s}	Subsidised sale price for rice or wheat
Q_i^{s}	Subsidised sales of rice or wheat
t_i, s_i	Domestic indirect tax and subsidy rates for commodity i
te_i, se_i	Export tax and subsidy rates for commodity i
tm_i, sm_i	Import tax and subsidy rates for commodity i
dt_h	Direct tax rate for household h
$k_i^{x}, \ k_i^{m}$	Export and import rationing factors for commodity i
C_G	Real government consumption
ω_h^{F}	Share of household group h in food subsidy
T_{Gh}	Transfer from government to households

Exogenous Variables

$FBOR$	Foreign borrowing
T_{Wh}, T_{hW}	Transfers between households and the rest of the world
$IRSUB$	Irrigation subsidy
S_i^{0}	Initial stocks of rice or wheat
ΔS_i	Change in stocks for commodity i
L_l^{0}	Initial employment for labour category l
w_l^{0}	Initial wage for labour category l
P_{0l}^{fd}	Initial value of food price index for labour category l
$PE_i^{w}, \ PM_i^{w}$	World prices of exports and imports
K_j	Capital stocks in sector j

Parameters

mr_i	Trade and transport margins
m_{ij}	Make matrix coefficients
a_{ij}	Input-output coefficients for non-agricultural activities
c_i	Base year share of output for commodity i (for price index)
μ_l^{fd}	Base year share of consumption for food commodity i for labour type l
a_{0i}, a_{1i}, a_{2i}	Parameters of procurement equation
st_i	Storage cost per unit for commodity i
pr_i	Procurement and distribution costs for commodity i
ρ_i	Mark-up above producer price for true retail price
F_j	Share of informal sector in value added in sector j
ϕ_{jl}	Share of labour of type l in wages paid by activity j
α_p	Neutral technical change parameter, $\alpha_p = 0$ for $p \notin A$, non-zero only for crop outputs
b_{pq}	Parameters of generalised quadratic supply/demand equations
ν_l	Elasticity of supply of labour with respect to real wage
η_l	Elasticity of wage adjustment with respect to food prices

$\tau_i,\ \gamma_i,\ \rho_i^T,\ \rho_i^M$	Trade aggregation parameters
mps_h	Savings rate for household h
$\gamma_{ih},\ \beta_{ih}$	LES demand equations parameters
W_{ih}	Share of commodity i in expenditure on commodities in C for household h
κ_{kj}	Share of capital of type k in gross profits from sector j
θ_{hl}^l	Share of household h in payments to labour of type l
θ_{hk}^K	Share of household h in payments to capital of type k
θ_h^M	Share of household h in income from self-employment
G_k	Share of government in payments to capital of type k
θ_k^R	Share of the rest of the world in payments to capital of type k
$S_i^{\ G}$	Share of government consumption allocated to commodity i
$S_i^{\ I}$	Share of investment demand allocated to commodity i
a_{ij}^{ag}	Input-output coefficients for agricultural commodities on a commodity by commodity basis

Bibliography

AHLUWALIA, I.J. (1979), "An Analysis of Price and Output Behavior in the Indian Economy: 1951-1973", *Journal of Development Economics*, Vol. 6.

ALI, I., B.M. DESAI, R. RADHAKRISHNA, and V.S. VYAS (1980), "India 2000: Agricultural Production Strategies and Rural Income Distribution", Indian Institute of Management, Ahmedabad, mimeo.

BINSWANGER, H., and J. QUIZON (1986), "Modeling the Impact of Agricultural Growth and Government Policy on Income Distribution in India", *World Bank Economic Review*, Vol. 1, No. 1, September.

BLYN, G. (1966), *Agricultural Trends in India, 1891-1947: Output, Availability, and Productivity*, University of Pennsylvania Press, Philadelphia.

DANTWALA, M.L. (1986), *Indian Agricultural Development Since Independence: A Collection of Essays*, Oxford & IBH Pub. Co., New Delhi.

DERVIS, K., J. de MELO and S. ROBINSON (1982), *General Equilibrium Models for Development Policy*, Cambridge University Press, New York.

GEORGE, P.S. (1988), "Costs and Benefits of Food Subsidies in India", in Pinstrup-Andersen, P., (ed.) *Food Subsidies in Developing Countries*, Johns Hopkins University Press, Baltimore.

GOLDIN, I., and O. KNUDSEN, eds, (1990), *Agricultural Trade Liberalization: Implications for Developing Countries*, OECD, Paris.

GULATI, A., with J. HANSON and G. PURSELL (1990), "Effective Incentives in India's Agriculture", Policy, Planning and Research Working Paper No. 332 (Trade Policy), The World Bank, January.

GULATI, A., and P.K. SHARMA (1990a), "Fertilizer Pricing and Subsidy: an Alternative Perspective", paper presented at National Workshop on Agricultural Input Marketing, Indian Institute of Management, Ahmedabad, Feb. 15-16.

GULATI, A., and P.K. SHARMA (1990b), "Prices, Procurement and Production: An Analysis of Wheat and Rice", *Economic and Political Weekly*, Vol. 25, No. 13, March 31.

GULATI, A., and P.K. SHARMA (1990c), "Employment, Foreign Exchange and Environment: Implications for Cropping Pattern", *Economic and Political Weekly*, Sept. 29.

GULATI, A., and P.K. SHARMA (1991), "Government Intervention in Agricultural Markets: Nature, Impact and Implications", *Journal of Indian School of Political Economy*, Vol. 3, No. 2.

HAYAMI, Y., K. SUBBARAO and K. OTSUKA, "Efficiency and Equity in Producer Levy of India", *American Journal of Agricultural Economics*, Vol. 64.

HERTEL, T.W. (1990), "Agricultural Trade Liberalization and the Developing Countries: A Survey of the Models", in Goldin, *et al. (1990).*

DE JANVRY, A., and K. SUBBARAO (1986), *Agricultural Price Policy and Income Distribution in India*, Oxford, New Delhi.

KAHLON, A.S. (1986), "Agricultural Price Policy and Terms of Trade", in Dantwala (1986).

KRUEGER, A.O., M. SCHIFF and A. VALDÉS, eds, (1991), *The Political Economy of Agricultural Pricing Policy*, Johns Hopkins University Press, Baltimore.

MAUNDER, A. and A. VALDÉS, eds, (1989), *Agriculture and Governments in an Interdependent World*, International Association of Agricultural Economists.

MITRA, A. (1977), *Terms of Trade and Class Relations*, Frank Cass, London.

NARAYANA, N.S.S., K. PARIKH and T.N SRINIVASAN (1991), *Agriculture, Growth, and Redistribution of Income: Policy Analysis with a General Equilibrium Model of India*, North Holland, New York.

NATIONAL COUNCIL OF APPLIED ECONOMIC RESEARCH (1980), *Household Income and its Distribution*, New Delhi.

PANDA, M. and H. SARKAR (1990), "Resource Mobilization through Administered Prices in an Indian CGE", in Taylor (1990).

PARIKH, K.S., *et al.*, (1988), *Toward Free Trade in Agriculture*, Nijhoff, Boston.

PLANNING COMMISSION (1981), *A Technical Note on the Sixth Plan of India (1980-85)*, Perspective Planning Division, Planning Commission, Government of India.

RADHAKRISHNA, R. and K.N. MURTY (1980), "Models of Complete Expenditure Systems for India", Working Paper No. 80-98, International Institute for Applied Systems Analysis, Laxenburg, Austria, May.

RANGARAJAN, C. (1982), "Agricultural Growth and Industrial Performance in India", Research Report No. 33, International Food Policy Research Institute, October.

RAO, C.H.H., S.K. RAY and K. SUBBARAO (1988), *Unstable Agriculture and Droughts*, Vikas, New Delhi.

RATTSO, J. (1990), "Conflicting Claims and Dynamic Inflation Mechanisms in India", in Taylor (1990).

SARMA J.S., and V.P. GANDHI (1990), "Production and Consumption of Food Grains in India: Implications of Accelerated Economic Growth and Poverty Alleviation", Research Report No. 81, International Food Policy Research Institute, July.

SUBBARAO, K. (1986), "Farm Prices: A Survey of the Debate," in Dantwala (1986).

SUBBARAO, K. (1991), "Pricing and Technology in Agriculture", mimeo, World Bank, Washington, D.C.

TAYLOR, L., ed., (1990), *Socially Relevant Policy Analysis: Structuralist Computable General Equilibrium Models for the Developing World*, MIT Press, Cambridge.

THE WORLD BANK (1989), *India: An Industrializing Economy in Transition*, Washington, D.C.

Table 1. **Pre- and Post-green Revolution Period Growth Rates (per cent) in Crop Production, Crop Area and Yield: All India**

Crops	Production			Area			Yield		
	1950-65	1966-88	1968-88	1950-65	1966-88	1968-88	1950-65	1966-88	1968-88
Rice	3.06	2.77	2.59	1.28	0.59	0.53	1.75	2.17	2.05
Wheat	3.57	5.69	5.03	2.32	2.30	1.88	1.22	3.32	3.09
Coarse Cereals	1.98	0.59	0.56	0.58	-0.90	-0.93	1.39	1.50	1.51
All Cereals	2.75	2.98	2.77	1.07	0.28	0.18	1.66	2.69	2.58
Pulses	1.12	0.81	0.70	1.60	0.21	0.23	-0.48	0.60	0.46
Oilseeds	2.70	2.96	2.99	2.40	1.32	1.37	0.29	1.62	1.60

Source: Computed from data in *Growth Rates in Agriculture, Area and Production of Principal Crops in India, 1985-86, Fertiliser Statistics*, 1986, 1987, 1988, 1989.

Table 2. **Pre- and Post-green Revolution Period Growth Rates (per cent) in Crop Production, Area and Yield: All India**
(Adjusted for Variations in Rainfall)

Crops	Production			Area			Yield		
	1950-65	1966-88	1968-88	1950-65	1966-88	1968-88	1950-65	1966-88	1968-88
Rice	3.34	2.60	2.42	1.31	0.68	0.67	2.03	1.92	1.75
Wheat	4.02	6.40	5.53	2.76	2.95	2.54	1.26	3.45	2.99
Coarse Cereals	2.17	0.85	0.85	0.88	-0.88	-0.94	1.28	1.65	1.75
All Cereals	3.17	3.07	2.88	1.28	0.42	0.35	1.66	2.20	2.10
Pulses	1.16	0.55	0.69	1.72	0.29	0.47	0.28	0.33	0.26
Oilseeds	2.04	1.75	1.63	0.14	0.86	1.44	-0.10	1.61	1.40
All Crops	3.02	2.72	2.63	1.60	0.46	0.47	1.26	2.00	1.89

Source: Rao *et al.*, Tables 2.1 and 4.1.

Table 3. **Composition of Regions and Regional Shares in Foodgrain Production, 1988/89**

Region	States and Union Territories	Share[1] of Population	Share of Foodgrain Production	Relative Share of Crops in Foodgrain Production			
				Wheat	Rice	Coarse Cereals & Pulses	Total
				(per cent)			
Northern	Punjab, Haryana, Jammu and Kashmir, Himachal Pradesh, Delhi, Chandigarh	6.8	17.1	64	24	12	100
Uttar Pradesh	Uttar Pradesh	16.2	21.0	55	27	18	100
Central	Madhya Pradesh, Rajasthan	12.6	15.6	32	19	48	100
Western	Maharashtra, Karnataka Gujarat, Goa, Daman and Diu, Dadra and Nagar Haveli	19.7	13.7	12	26	62	100
Eastern	Bihar, West Bengal, Orissa, Assam, Tripura, Manipur, Meghalaya, Arunachal Pradesh, Nagaland, Sikkim, Mizoram, Andaman and Nicobar Is.	26.0	20.1	13	75	12	100
Southern	Andhra Pradesh, Tamil Nadu, Kerala, Pondicherry, Lakshwadweep	18.7	12.6	0	81	19	100

1. Population shares are for 1981; 1991 census data are not available yet.
Source: Sarma and Gandhi (1990) Table 4 for population data. Crop shares etc. computed from data in Fertiliser Statistics, 1989/90.

Table 4. Regional Foodgrain Yields and Area and Input Shares (1980 and 1988)

Region	Foodgrain Yield (kg/ha)		Share of Gross Cropped Area		Share of Area under Foodgrains		High-yielding Varieties				Fertilizer Consumption				Irrigated Area			
							Share of Total Area		Extent of Adoption		Share of Total		Intensity		Share of Total		As Fraction of Cropped Area	
	1980-81	1988-89	1980-81	1986-87	1980-81	1989-90	1980-81	1989-90	1980-81	1989-90	1980-81	1989-90	1980-81	1986-87	1980-81	1986-87	1980-81	1986-87
	(kg/ha)						(per cent)						(kg/ha)		(per cent)			
Northern	1 940	2 547	7.8	8.4	8.4	8.9	16.2	14.5	75.8	83.8	19.1	15.2	72.2	118.2	19.6	20.0	68.1	74.4
Uttar Pradesh	1 219	1 725	16.0	15.2	16.2	16.2	20.5	20.9	46.0	70.6	21.3	19.4	46.8	83.0	22.9	23.2	46.3	47.6
Central	627	865	22.1	22.3	22.1	23.9	11.7	14.9	19.2	39.1	6.2	8.5	8.6	24.7	12.5	14.0	16.0	19.6
Western	803	882	23.0	23.9	19.9	20.6	19.2	19.5	37.1	56.7	20.9	22.8	26.9	61.9	13.2	13.4	15.6	17.4
Eastern	1 061	1 301	19.0	18.4	20.9	20.5	17.9	18.4	31.4	48.6	10.8	12.4	18.0	43.7	15.6	15.6	23.9	26.3
Southern	1 227	1 675	12.1	11.8	10.9	10.0	14.5	11.8	49.7	68.4	21.8	21.7	54.3	119.6	16.2	21.7	37.2	36.3
All India	1 023	1 327							44.0	57.3			31.8	65.0			28.6	31.1

Source: Fertiliser Statistics, various issues, and Sarma and Gandhi (1990), Table 6 for the 1980 figures.

Table 5. Regional Growth Rates of Area, Production and Yield, 1952/53-1988/89
(per cent per year)

Region	Rice			Wheat			Coarse Cereals			Total Cereals			Pulses			All Foodgrains		
	Area	Prod-uction	Yield	Area	Prod-uction	Yield	Area	Prod-uction	Yield	Area	Prod-uction	Yield	Area	Prod-uction	Yield	Area	Prod-uction	Yield
Northern																		
1952/53-1964/65	4.64	5.99	1.29	3.30	5.25	1.89	-0.17	2.45	2.62	1.84	4.39	2.52	1.37	1.23	-0.14	1.64	3.58	1.91
1967/68-1975/76	4.54	10.24	5.45	2.75	4.49	1.69	0.21	0.85	0.65	1.98	4.38	2.36	-1.98	-5.77	-3.85	1.26	3.30	2.02
1975/76-1988/89	6.07	7.92	1.74	2.17	5.65	3.40	-3.21	-2.10	1.14	1.58	5.20	3.57	-6.37	-7.79	-1.52	0.67	4.62	3.94
Uttar Pradesh																		
1952/53-1964/65	1.83	4.29	2.42	0.84	1.54	0.70	-0.93	-0.61	0.33	0.38	1.46	1.08	0.53	-1.20	-1.72	0.42	0.79	0.37
1967/68-1975/76	0.22	2.90	2.66	2.86	3.14	0.27	-1.87	-1.74	0.13	0.44	1.69	1.25	-3.51	-5.36	-1.92	-0.32	0.52	0.84
1975/76-1988/89	0.87	5.76	4.85	2.27	5.23	3.88	-2.62	0.14	2.83	0.63	5.03	4.37	-0.13	0.92	1.05	0.52	4.60	4.06
Central																		
1952/53-1964/65	1.30	2.17	0.86	3.49	2.74	-0.73	1.30	2.27	0.95	1.72	2.34	0.60	2.08	2.62	0.53	1.82	2.38	0.56
1967/68-1975/76	1.12	0.57	-0.54	2.08	5.02	2.88	-1.34	-0.72	0.63	-0.08	1.26	1.34	2.61	4.09	1.43	0.66	1.84	1.17
1975/76-1988/89	0.42	2.90	2.47	0.16	4.16	3.99	0.54	1.52	0.97	0.42	2.90	2.47	-1.32	-0.53	0.80	-0.07	2.23	2.30
Western																		
1952/53-1964/65	1.87	4.29	2.38	1.19	3.48	2.28	0.01	2.41	2.41	0.34	2.98	2.63	-0.34	-0.27	0.07	0.22	2.59	2.37
1967/68-1975/76	-0.43	1.38	1.82	1.75	8.24	6.39	-1.20	1.57	2.82	-0.84	2.22	3.09	1.86	3.56	1.68	-0.39	2.36	2.76
1975/76-1988/89	0.19	0.02	0.17	-3.85	-3.35	0.53	-0.23	-0.55	-0.33	-0.49	-0.67	-0.19	1.38	2.44	1.05	-0.13	-0.37	-0.25
Eastern																		
1952/53-1964/65	0.69	2.19	1.49	0.71	2.23	1.51	0.72	2.21	1.48	0.70	2.20	1.49	0.57	1.10	0.52	0.68	2.07	1.38
1967/68-1975/76	0.72	0.64	-0.08	9.61	15.11	5.01	-0.11	-2.26	-2.16	1.33	1.73	0.41	0.60	-2.66	-3.24	1.23	1.39	0.15
1975/76-1988/89	0.00	2.14	2.13	0.00	1.39	1.38	-2.53	0.58	3.18	-0.22	1.92	2.15	0.40	2.50	2.09	-0.14	1.96	2.10
Southern																		
1952/53-1964/65	2.62	4.64	1.96	1.61	1.15	-0.46	-0.60	2.12	2.74	0.87	3.82	2.92	0.28	-0.18	-0.46	0.79	3.67	2.84
1967/68-1975/76	0.46	2.88	2.40	9.24	28.94	18.02	-0.58	1.62	2.21	-0.03	2.56	2.58	1.79	6.07	4.21	0.20	2.66	2.46
1975/76-1988/89	-1.35	1.64	3.03	-6.57	-7.25	-0.73	-3.69	-2.58	1.15	-2.37	0.68	3.12	1.85	5.77	3.85	-1.72	0.88	2.65
All India																		
1952/53-1964/65	1.57	3.34	1.74	2.29	3.32	1.02	0.21	1.38	1.16	0.99	2.63	1.62	1.36	0.62	-0.73	1.07	2.33	1.25
1967/68-1975/76	0.67	1.89	1.21	3.20	5.47	2.18	-1.07	0.27	1.35	0.31	2.22	1.90	0.77	-0.51	-1.27	0.40	1.91	1.50
1975/76-1988/89	0.25	2.76	2.45	0.96	4.64	3.52	-0.99	-0.38	0.63	-0.09	2.59	2.61	-0.28	0.63	0.91	-0.13	2.41	2.47

Source: Sarma and Gandhi (1990), Table 6, for growth rates up to 1975/76.
Growth rates for 1975-1988 are based on data from *Area and Production of Principal Crops in India, 1985-86* and *Fertiliser Statistics, 1987-88, 1988-89* and *1989-90.*

Table 6. Marketed Surplus as Fraction of Production (various years)
and Share of Production (1988-89)
(per cent)

State	Rice			Wheat			Sorghum		
	1979-80	1980-81	Share[1]	1981-82	1982-83	Share[1]	1981-82	1982-83	Share[1]
Andhra Pradesh	39.1	41.4	14.9	...	...	...	11.3	8.4	7.1
Bihar	15.0	15.8	8.7	8.1	12.2	11.3	...	...	...
Gujarat	41.2	41.3	1.2	36.4	39.4	2.8	24.6	29.6	4.0
Haryana	85.6	93.2	2.0	32.6	40.5	11.8	...	...	...
Karnataka	17.9	18.1	3.4	9.0	9.4	0.3	2.9	4.6	14.4
Kerala	19.5	29.6	1.4	...	...	...	...	...	...
Madhya Pradesh	21.3	21.5	6.9	8.7	11.0	8.6	9.3	9.4	17.9
Maharashtra	10.9	14.4	3.8	21.9	29.9	1.9	15.7	14.8	40.7
Orissa	4.0	3.6	7.5	...	...	...	...	...	...
Punjab	97.0	93.1	7.0	54.4	53.4	21.4	...	...	...
Rajasthan	30.0	33.3	0.3	20.4	18.9	7.3	13.2	12.7	5.1
Tamil Nadu	33.6	36.1	7.9	...	...	...	11.7	7.0	5.3
Uttar Pradesh	29.4	29.6	13.6	15.2	15.6	36.5	13.0	10.1	4.7
West Bengal	19.5	18.4	14.9	...	...	...	...	...	...

1. Share in all-India crop output in 1988-89.
Source: Bulletin on Food Statistics, 1987-89. Output shares for 1988-89 computed from Fertiliser Statistics, 1989-90.

Table 7. **Input Structure of Wheat (average of 1981-82 to 1983-84)**

(per cent)

Items	Haryana	Madhya Pradesh	Punjab	Uttar Pradesh
Operational Cost	66.95	53.82	60.70	67.58
Human Labour	16.80	13.89	14.64	16.47
Bullock Labour	7.81	10.92	3.00	13.87
Machine Labour	10.54	2.44	12.37	7.42
Seed	7.84	10.80	4.57	6.51
Fertilizer	13.42	7.40	19.36	13.68
Manure	0.16	0.37	0.36	1.36
Insecticide	1.27	0.01	1.55	0.04
Irrigation Charges	7.45	6.53	3.02	6.47
Interest on Working Capital	1.72	1.43	1.66	1.72
Miscellaneous	--	--	0.18	--
Fixed Costs	33.50	46.18	39.30	32.42
Rental Value of Owned Land	21.08	33.07	23.29	21.75
Rent Paid for Leased-in Land	1.25	0.16	5.67	0.88
Land Revenue, Cesses, Taxes	0.25	0.31	0.08	0.38
Depreciation on Implements and Farm Buildings	1.70	4.22	1.82	2.22
Interest on Fixed Capital	8.77	8.40	8.44	7.16
Total Cost (Rs/ha)	100.00 (3 790.08)	100.00 (2 977.88)	100.00 (4 057.98)	100.00 (3 681.87)
Cost (Rs/quintal)	132.75	134.95	127.26	134.72
Procurement Price (Rs/quintal)	148.33	148.33	148.33	148.33
Procurement Price ($/MT)[1]	160.00	160.00	160.00	160.00
World Price (Rs/quintal)[1]	152.87	152.87	152.87	152.87
World Price ($/MT)[1]	164.89	164.89	164.89	164.89

1. World price is for US Hard Red Winter No. 2 (fob Gulf ports) as reported in Gulati *et al.* (1990), Annex 2. The conversion to rupees uses the average exchange rate reported therein.
Source: Gulati *et al.* (1990), Annex 11.

Table 7 (Continued). **Input Structure of Rice (average of 1981-82 to 1983-84)**
(per cent)

Items	Andhra Pradesh	Bihar	Madhya Pradesh	Orissa	Punjab	Uttar Pradesh
Operational Cost	65.47	51.51	57.39	61.03	63.87	63.25
Human Labour	25.53	24.85	22.93	29.20	20.09	26.42
Bullock Labour	7.16	13.36	15.91	14.52	2.26	13.76
Machine Labour	2.65	0.11	0.10	0.02	6.67	1.63
Seed	3.37	4.24	8.54	6.54	2.19	5.62
Fertilizer	15.24	4.97	5.72	3.44	15.41	8.07
Manure	4.12	1.04	2.42	5.02	1.46	2.41
Insecticide	1.81	0.02	0.33	0.28	2.09	0.14
Irrigation Charges	3.67	0.74	0.16	0.54	11.94	3.72
Interest on Working Capital	1.89	1.19	1.39	1.46	1.74	1.47
Fixed Costs	34.53	48.49	42.61	38.97	36.13	36.75
Rental Value of Owned Land	29.05	41.09	--	25.40	23.43	24.41
Rent Paid for Leased-in Land	0.38	0.26	32.02	7.08	4.60	0.90
Land Revenue, Cesses, Taxes	0.63	0.88	0.13	0.28	0.06	0.47
Depreciation on Implements and Farm Buildings	1.54	1.00	4.31	2.04	1.35	2.51
Interest on Fixed Capital	3.05	5.23	6.09	4.17	6.69	8.47
Total Cost	100.00	100.00	100.00	100.00	100.00	100.00
(Rs/ha)	(4 519.15)	(2 569.71)	(1 695.90)	(2 376.25)	(5 920.70)	(2 851.21)
Cost (Rs/quintal)	(125.09)	(125.25)	(106.95)	(115.39)	(109.50)	(117.46)
Procurement Price (Rs/quintal)	203.12	195.60	199.65	203.90	206.43	194.68
Procurement Price ($/MT)[1]	209.68	201.92	206.10	210.49	213.10	200.97
World Price (Rs/quintal)[1]	300.54	300.54	300.54	300.54	300.54	300.54
World Price ($/MT)[1]	310.25	310.25	310.25	310.25	310.25	310.25

1. World price is for Thai white (milled) 5 per cent broken (fob Bangkok) as reported in Gulati *et al.* (1990), Annex 4. The conversion to rupees uses the average exchange rate reported therein.
Source: Gulati *et al.* (1990), Annex 12.

Table 8. Labour Absorption (Man-days/Ha) for Major Crops and States

Crops	Andhra Pradesh	Assam	Bihar	Gujarat	Haryana	Himachal Pradesh	Karnataka	Madhya Pradesh	Maharashtra	Orissa	Punjab	Rajasthan	Tamil Nadu	Uttar Pradesh	West Bengal
Paddy	150.58	81.47	107.31	-	83.51	-	125.79	72.26	-	126.06	104.77	-	159.36	108.8	129.19
Wheat	-	-	92.02	-	48.63	43.36	-	45.87	-	-	51.54	73.52	-	77.34	-
Maize	-	-	115.71	-	-	61.90	-	60.34	-	-	-	81.94	-	-	-
Jowar	50.09	-	-	59.57	-	-	52.33	50.32	72.03	-	-	-	-	-	-
Bajra	-	-	-	85.62	42.29	-	-	-	-	-	-	29.55	-	69.47	-
Barley	-	-	-	-	-	-	-	-	-	-	-	70.76	-	-	-
Ragi	-	-	-	-	-	-	87.39	-	-	-	-	-	132.75	-	-
Gram	-	-	-	-	24.91	-	-	40.39	-	-	-	31.26	-	64.87	-
Urad	41.59	-	-	-	-	-	-	51.04	-	44.95	-	-	54.65	67.27	-
Tur	-	-	-	-	-	-	47.75	75.93	-	-	-	-	-	88.13	-
Moong	54.59	-	-	-	-	-	-	47.69	-	45.67	-	36.71	-	62.20	-
Mustard	-	71.88	-	-	34.47	-	-	-	-	-	-	43.70	-	-	-
Groundnut	86.26	-	-	61.37	-	-	73.26	63.84	-	136.01	-	-	105.88	-	-
Soybean	-	-	-	-	-	-	-	51.92	-	-	-	-	-	-	-
Sunflower	-	-	-	-	-	-	38.62	43.31	45.16	-	-	-	-	46.10	-
Cotton	-	-	-	129.17	-	-	95.49	66.89	91.79	-	101.27	-	-	-	197.77
Jute	-	182.45	102.00	-	-	-	-	-	-	196.62	-	-	-	-	-
Sugarcane	344.88	-	122.41	-	127.26	-	215.83	-	376.49	-	-	-	332.54	137.45	-

Source: Gulati and Sharma (1990c), Table 2.

94

Table 9. **Unit Costs, Support Prices and Market Prices
in High and Low Productivity Regions, Wheat and Rice**

State	Year	Yield	Unit Cost	Farm Harvest Price	Support Price	World Price
		(quintal/ha)		(Rs/quintal)		
Wheat						
High Productivity Regions						
Punjab	1983-84	29.5	137.5	141	152	158.83
	1984-85	33.5	136.3	-	157	169.86
	1985-86	35.6	129.3	-	162	173.33
Haryana	1983-84	25.6	140.9	-	152	158.83
	1984-85	26.5	141.3	-	157	169.86
	1985-86	31.2	125.6	-	162	173.33
Low Productivity Regions						
Madhya Pradesh	1981-82	-	132.7	201	142	148.12
	1982-83	-	-	178	151	151.65
	1983-84	-	140.2	173	152	158.83
Paddy						
High Productivity Regions						
Andhra Pradesh	1983-84	33.9	141	149	132	194.03
Punjab	1983-84	52.8	122	133	132	194.03
Low Productivity Regions						
Bihar	1983-84	18.7	133	175	132	194.03
W. Bengal	1983-84	27.0	123	173	132	194.03

1. World price for wheat is for US Hard Winter No. 2 (fob Gulf ports) and for rice, for Thai White (milled) 5 per cent broken, from Annexes 2 and 4 of Gulati *et al.* (1990), converted to rupees using the exchange rates therein. The paddy-to-rice conversion ratio is assumed to be 2/3.

Source: Subbarao (1991), Table 5.

Table 10. Subsidies on Wheat and Rice

Years	Total Consumer Subsidy	Total Carrying Cost	Total Subsidy on Wheat and Rice (2)+(3)	Per Unit Subsidy		Per Unit Subsidy as Fraction of Procurement Price	
				Wheat	Rice	Wheat	Rice
(1)	(2)	(3)	(4)	(5)	(6)	(7)	(8)
	(Rs million)			(Rs/quintal)		(per cent)	
1980-81	4 854.0	1 760.8	6 614.8	40.19	34.02	34.35	21.60
1981-82	6 224.1	1 548.1	7 772.2	53.73	42.94	41.33	24.89
1982-83	7 596.2	1 844.7	9 440.9	55.4	53.35	39.01	29.15
1983-84	8 222.4	2 689.9	10 912.3	49.07	66.70	32.50	33.69
1984-85	8 547.4	4 979.4	13 526.8	63.46	74.87	41.75	36.43
1985-86	13 733.9	5 175.7	18 909.6	69.57	77.34	44.31	36.31
1986-87	16 225.9	5 100.5	21 326.4	84.93	80.47	52.43	36.74
1987-88	19 243.3	2 038.2	21 281.5	82.79	80.94	49.87	35.97
1988-89	17 451.0	1 140.9	18 591.9	78.21	81.73	45.21	34.05
1989-90	17 742.0	1 672.2	19 414.2	106.9	124.23	58.42	44.77

Source: Gulati and Sharma (1991), Table 3.

Table 11. Social Accounting Matrix for India
(1983-84, Rs Million)

	ACTIVITIES																		COMMODITIES
	Rice	Wheat	Coarse Cereals	Other Crops	Dairy Products	Meat	Edible Oils	Sugar	Other Foods	Textiles	Consumer Gds.	Intermed-iates	Durables	Services	Public Admin.	Draught Animal Svc	Fertilizer	All Activities	Rice
ACTIVITIES																			
Rice																			168327
Wheat																			464
Coarse Cereals																			
Other Crops																			124
Dairy Products																			
Meat																			
Edible Oils																			
Sugar																			
Other Foods																			
Textiles																			
Consumer Gds.																			
Intermediates																			
Durables																			
Services																			
Public Admin.																			
Draught Animal Svc																			
Fertilizer																			
All Activities																			168914
COMMODITIES																			
Rice	16137	19		49		1077	106		895	35		1242	1	5487		3	3	25048	
Wheat	12	10675		107	508	1359	2		2467	12		32	1	3145				18315	
Coarse Cereals	148	9	557	60	53	2550	15		712			2						391	
Other Crops		292		16912	18975	25341	42724	18857	15246	21169		7410	44	6736		28444		202434	
Dairy Products				3664					9926			11		3723		134		13712	
Meat		350	924	10	50	3477	9	6	3183	2007		286	2	3805		61		18074	
Edible Oils				53			330	271	1297	1	136	2019	75	2524				19140	
Sugar							15		5197			175		889			746	6531	
Other Foods	157				2450		7215	561	10007	317	1651	666	1	2736				14803	
Textiles		47						3	401	57490	103	5905	24	1705			11	70119	
Consumer Gds.	945	772	544	1397	135	736		122	191	141	335	19696	514	191		53		24388	
Intermediates	6632	6063	2431	10271	1287	598		1248		36022	3568	382809	651	115079		210	14939	672853	
Durables	7245	4683	1526		336	544		323		2845	2940	31173	82119	39177	33510		353	125783	
Services	12413	6491	7826	8363		5742	6791	6156	14529	34793	567	121023	44154	143601		4449	5692	407047	
Public admin.																			
Draught Animal Svc.	2104			14700	8	342					5371		8				2347	41429	
Fertilizer	8598	6750	2157	8995	3572													29066	
All Commodities	54396	36155	15965	64581	27375	41788	61806	27545	74003	154834	14663	572658	161104	328799		33143	24098	1692913	
FACTORS																			
Ag. Wages	33593	13424	18465	39051	17160	2991										1692		126377	
Ag. Profits	102402	54760	33859	216260	66860	11653										6594		492386	
Non ag. Wages						2166	1488	3251	10975	41303	17946	139313	44859	233332	92382		1516	588531	
Non ag. Profits							929	2029	6851	25782	18682	86059	30648	138803			4549	314331	
Self-Employed						12275	679	1484	5010	18855	8237	50502	13325	226152				336520	
All Factors	135995	68184	52324	255312	84020	29084	3096	6764	22836	85940	44865	275874	88831	598287	92382	8286	6066	1858146	
HOUSEHOLDS																			
Landless																			
Small Farmers																			
Med Farmers																			
Lge Farmers																			
Workers																			
Marginals																			
Capitalists																			
All Households																			
Government																			-3023
Taxes																			
Capital																			
Stocks																			
Rest of World																			1004
Total	190391	104339	68289	319893	111395	70873	64902	34308	96839	240774	59529	848532	249935	927086	92382	41429	30164	3551058	166895

97

Table 11. Social Accounting Matrix for India (continued)
(1983/84, Rs Million)

Columns Wheat–All Commodities fall under the heading COMMODITIES; Wages and Ag. Profits fall under the heading FACTORS.

Account	Wheat	Coarse Cereals	Other Crops	Dairy Products	Meat	Edible Oils	Sugar	Other Foods	Textiles	Consumer Goods	Intermediates	Durables	Services	Public Admin.	Draught Animal Svc.	Fertil.	All Commodities	Wages	Ag. Profits
ACTIVITIES																			
Rice	40		22024										746				190391		
Wheat	88063		15813														104339		
Coarse Cereals		52079	16210														68289		
Other Crops	160		319609														319893		
Dairy Products				111395													111395		
Meat					70872												70872		
Edible Oils						61580		130			2605		548				64903		
Sugar						112	33391	316			53		528				34509		
Other Foods					28	189	94	92320	60		421	11	3853				96840		
Textiles									210919	4	278	9	29378				240777		
Consumer Gds								239	6	58321	429	28	28				59529		
Intermediates						1041		18	129	29	831866	5021	10032			164	848322		
Durables									53	30	3275	233536	13015			11	249938		
Services					94							8816	918168				927078		
Public Admin.														92382			92382		
Draught Animal Svc.															41427		41426		
Fertilizers											441		445			29278	30164		
All Activities	88263	52079	373655	111395	70994	62922	33485	93024	211167	58384	839367	247420	976714	92382	41427	29453	3551046		
COMMODITIES																			
Rice																			
Wheat																			
Coarse Cereals																			
Other Crops																			
Dairy Products																			
Meat																			
Edible Oils																			
Sugar																			
Other Foods																			
Textiles																			
Consumer Gds																			
Intermediates																			
Durables																			
Services																			
Public Admin.																			
Draught Animal Svc.																			
Fertilizers																			
All Commodities																			
FACTORS																			
Ag. Wages																			
Ag. Profits																			
Non ag. Wages																			
Non ag. Profits																			
Self-employed																			
All Factors																			
HOUSEHOLDS																			
Landless																		31126	3612
Small Farmers																		40139	62240
Med. Farmers																		29934	183570
Lge. Farmers																		25177	242965
Workers																			
Marginals																			
Capitalists																			
All Households																		126377	492386
Government																			
Taxes	-3869	-649	-1605	-134	88	1552	2474	29773	8473	2586	114999	62574	15929			-8499	220668		
Capital																			
Stocks																			
Rest of World	6710	7	2573		1233	7347		665	2001	254	100958	39218	12238			2045	176751		
Total	91104	51437	374623	111261	72314	71821	35959	123462	221641	61224	1055324	349212	1005581	92382	41427	22999	3948465	126377	492386

Table 11. Social Accounting Matrix for India (end)
(1983/84, Rs Million)

	FACTORS Non ag. Wages	Non ag. Profits	Self-employed	All Factors	HOUSEHOLDS Landless	Small Farmers	Medium Farmers	Large Farmers	Workers	Marginals	Capitalists	All Households	Government	Taxes	Capital	Stocks	Rest of World	Total
ACTIVITIES																		
Rice																		190391
Wheat																		104339
Coarse Cereals																		68289
Other Crops																		319893
Dairy Products																		111395
Meat																		70873
Edible Oils																		64902
Sugar																		34308
Other Foods																		96839
Textiles																		240774
Consumer Gds.																		59529
Intermediates																		848532
Durables																		249935
Services																		927086
Public Admin.																		92382
Draught Animal Svc.																		41429
Fertilizers																		30163
All Activities																		3551058
COMMODITIES																		
Rice					10534	32761	36967	16979	20798	11998	2339	132377	116			8396	958	166894
Wheat					3950	12284	18753	10470	13142	7504	1535	67639	111			5024	15	91104
Coarse Cereals					4910	15269	17035	6804	14436	1250	247	48961	154			501	3	51497
Other Crops					8388	25075	34617	23365	44190	19008	6643	61287	101	2072	3512	7237	374623
Dairy Products					1752	9914	19367	18974	31042	11531	4867	97447	12				111261
Meat					2256	4572	8383	6903	16047	6523	2576	47263			1872	3022	72314
Edible Oils					2048	7040	9668	6648	14849	6689	2041	48984			2347	1351	71821
Sugar					854	3083	11614	4012	4714	2247	650	27175			488	1764	35958
Other Foods					3197	5530	10443	9522	47518	4283	9778	100272	104		1729	6554	123462
Textiles					4520	7367	17960	35602	39490	10017	10386	125342	319	135	1064	4662	221641
Consumer Gds.					1119	2671	4982	5321	11112	3588	2239	31042	52		941	941	61224
Intermediates					4646	14365	17548	9920	19855	9507	2894	78736	30770	214248	23612	35108	1055324
Durables					1251	1062	3240	8774	8081	2170	5826	30404	15747	149194	5221	36213	349212
Services					15328	38227	67850	69440	184682	59786	37792	473106	71472	17545			1005381
Public Admin.													92382					92382
Draught Animal Svc.																		41427
Fertilizers													67					42999
All Commodities					64753	179220	278428	232735	459936	166116	89816	1471004	211407	383194	58567	131386	3948465
FACTORS																		
Ag. Wages																		126377
Ag. Profits																		492386
Non ag. Wages																		588531
Non ag. Profits																		319118
Self-employed																		336520
All Factors																		1862932
HOUSEHOLDS																		
Landless	1757	2414	22576	61485									2851	195			7395	71927
Small Farmers	4383	6035	56443	169239									8023	486			6999	184748
Med. Farmers	4638	7523	70351	286015									8582	862			3809	309268
Lge. Farmers		4543	42481	315166									13091	881			2963	332101
Workers	577753			577753									22502	6035			3789	610080
Marginals		15470	144669	160139									15520	3071			1563	180293
Capitalists		170955		170955									1321	479			1332	185987
All Households	588531	206940	336520	1750754									83790	12009		110	27850	1874403
Government		97378		97378									69444	267269				364641
Taxes																		279278
Capital		14800		14800								344679						441761
Stocks															58567			58567
Rest of World				4780									27640					191656
Total	588531	319118	336520	1862932	71927	184748	309268	332101	610080	180293	185987	1874403	364641	279278	441761	58567	191656	

99

Table 12. **Household Incomes, Savings and Sources of Income**

| | Population (thousand) | Per Capita Income (Rs) | Expenditure (Rs) | Savings (Rs) | Sources of Income (per cent) | | | | | | | |
					Govern-ment	Rest of World	Agric. Wage	Agric. Profit	Non-agric. Wage	Non-agric. Profit	Self-Employment	Food Subsidy
Rural Households												
Landless	60 245	1 190.7	1 071.6	119.1	3.97	10.31	43.39	5.03	2.45	3.37	31.47	0.0
Small farmers	169 545	1 086.8	1 054.2	32.6	4.35	3.80	21.78	33.78	2.38	3.28	30.63	0.0
Medium farmers	181 352	1 700.6	1 530.5	170.1	2.78	1.24	9.71	59.52	1.50	2.44	22.81	0.0
Large farmers	79 103	4 187.2	2 931.0	1 256.2	3.95	0.89	7.60	73.35	0.0	1.37	12.83	0.0
All rural	490 245	1 826.9	1 535.4	291.5								
Urban Households												
Worker	127 208	4 777.5	3 650.6	1 126.9	3.70	0.62	0.0	0.0	95.07	0.0	0.0	0.61
Marginal	79 659	2 253.8	2 075.8	178.0	8.64	0.87	0.0	0.0	0.0	8.62	80.58	1.29
Capitalist	17 486	10 608.9	8 078.9	2 530.0	7.13	0.72	0.0	0.0	0.0	92.16	0.0	0.0
All urban	224 353	4 335.9	3 436.6	899.3								

Source: Computed.

Table 13. **Agricultural Supply and Input Demand Elasticities**

a) unadjusted

Item	Price						
	Draught Animal Services	Fertilizer	Rice	Wheat	Coarse Cereals	Other Crops	Agricultural Labour
Draught Animal Services	-0.404	0.0	0.0	0.0	0.0	0.0	0.133
Fertilizer	0.0	-0.835	0.003	0.120	-0.463	0.752	0.428
Rice	0.0	-0.021	0.553	-0.128	-0.127	-0.183	-0.094
Wheat	0.0	-0.061	-0.090	0.445	-0.158	-0.088	-0.048
Coarse Cereals	0.0	0.179	-0.228	-0.109	0.755	-0.204	-0.399
Other Crops	0.0	-0.101	-0.163	-0.032	-0.065	0.295	0.066
Agricultural Labour	0.122	0.075	0.102	0.023	0.204	-0.049	-0.478

b) adjusted

Item	Price						
	Draught Animal Services	Fertilizer	Rice	Wheat	Coarse Cereals	Other Crops	Agricultural Labour
Draught Animal Services	-0.404	-0.040	0.0	0.0	0.0	0.0	0.444
Fertilizer	-0.063	-0.836	0.129	0.200	-0.351	0.758	0.162
Rice	0.0	-0.020	0.553	-0.047	-0.071	-0.364	-0.052
Wheat	0.0	-0.061	-0.090	0.445	-0.023	-0.243	-0.028
Coarse Cereals	0.0	0.179	-0.228	-0.039	0.755	-0.256	-0.412
Other Crops	0.0	-0.054	-0.163	-0.056	-0.036	0.295	0.014
Agricultural Labour	0.176	0.041	0.083	0.023	0.204	-0.049	-0.478

Source: Unadjusted elasticities from Binswanger and Quizon (1986); adjusted elasticities: computed.

Table 14. **Structure of Trade and Production (1983-84)**

	Trade Ratios[1]		Actual Tariffs		NPC		Share in Total			Substitution Elasticity	
	Imports	Exports	Imports	Exports	Imports	Exports	Output	Imports	Exports	Imports	Exports
	(per cent)							(per cent)			
Rice	0.64	0.66	...	...	0.700	0.890	4.89	0.57	0.89	15	10
Wheat	7.80	0.02	...	-0.013	0.840	1.290	2.48	3.80	0.01	15	8
Coarse Cereals	0.01	0.01	...	...	...	...	1.46	...	...	...	...
Other Crops	0.70	2.08	0.308	-0.065	1.200	...	10.49	1.45	6.09	1.2	1.0
Dairy Products	...	...	...	...	...	...	3.14	...	...	...	...
Meat, Fish & Eggs	1.83	4.45	0.178	-0.044	...	...	2.00	0.70	2.49	1.5	1.5
Edible Oils & Fats	11.02	2.36	0.057	-0.090	1.800	...	1.77	4.16	1.17	3	3
Sugar	...	7.06	...	-0.254	1.150	...	0.94	...	1.86	4	4
Other Foods	0.78	6.69	0.110	0.054	1.150	...	2.62	0.38	4.90	1.1	1.0
Clothing	1.07	7.40	0.188	-0.062	1.300	...	5.94	1.13	12.30	4	1.5
Consumer Goods	0.48	8.38	0.211	-0.059	1.000	...	1.64	0.14	3.85	3	1.2
Intermediates	11.29	4.31	0.262	-0.029	1.271	...	23.61	57.12	28.46	1.2	0.5
Durables	14.12	8.42	0.679	-0.045	1.870	...	6.96	22.19	16.39	1.1	0.5
Services	1.32	2.81	...	-0.025	...	...	27.47	7.21	21.57	0.5	0.5
Public Admin.	...	...	...	...	...	...	2.60	...	...	...	...
Draught Animal Services	...	...	...	...	...	...	1.16	...	...	...	...
Fertilizer	5.42	0.02	-0.196	...	...	...	0.83	1.16	...	4	3

1. Share of imports in absorption and share of exports in production, respectively.
Source: See text.

Table 15. **Scenarios 1 and 2: Trade Liberalisation in India**
(Changes from base-year levels, per cent)

		In Agriculture				Economy-wide	
		1A		1B		2	
		1	2	1	2	1	2
AGGREGATES	GDP	0.77	0.29	1.47	0.22	-3.25	-0.15
	Investment	0.62	0.27	1.54	0.63	0.38	2.65
	Exports	5.55	4.91	12.59	10.86	57.95	62.98
	Imports	4.16	3.69	10.34	9.06	51.96	55.63
	Agricultural Exports	30.39	30.85	38.21	39.72	163.86	154.30
	Non-agric. Exports	1.23	0.40	8.14	5.85	39.55	47.11
	Agricultural Imports	35.21	33.50	88.43	83.49	41.71	50.46
	Non-agric. Imports	0.57	0.25	1.32	0.47	53.14	56.23
	Exchange Rate	0.32	0.22	3.60	3.33	26.80	27.33
	Government Revenue	0.00	-0.00	0.00	0.00	0.00	-0.00
	Government Savings	0.15	0.52	0.79	1.80	4.78	2.62
	Food Subsidy	-5.95	-6.81	-9.73	-12.03	-7.86	-0.42
	Fertilizer	-0.39	-0.83	-0.04	-1.08	6.09	8.40
	Consumer	10.87	9.14	19.11	14.45	82.56	96.73
	Total Subsidies	-0.18	-0.66	-0.98	-2.22	-5.92	-3.26
	Terms of Trade	-0.00	-0.51	-0.30	-1.66	5.00	9.03
RICE	Exports	590.52	602.55	735.72	773.26	1765.99	1605.64
	Imports	69.85	65.29	28.48	19.81	-64.30	-58.57
	Output	2.62	2.65	3.78	3.89	8.18	7.53
	Price	3.11	2.81	4.13	3.35	15.44	17.33
WHEAT	Imports	0.41	-1.82	-15.84	-21.15	-84.99	-79.46
	Output	0.22	0.25	1.18	1.24	2.24	2.38
	Price	0.25	-0.01	1.91	1.20	10.92	13.64
COARSE CEREALS	Output	0.03	-0.07	0.23	0.03	-1.09	-0.91
	Price	0.63	0.47	0.58	0.01	3.21	5.94

Table 15. (continued)

| | | In Agriculture | | | | Economy-wide | |
| | | 1A | | 1B | | 2 | |
		1	2	1	2	1	2
OTHER CROPS	Exports	-5.23	-4.89	-1.33	-0.40	14.91	11.97
	Imports	233.15	231.06	211.30	206.21	145.51	156.76
	Output	-1.15	-1.23	-1.92	-2.13	-3.89	-3.38
	Price	-2.84	-3.36	-4.37	-5.70	-1.53	2.03
EDIBLE OILS	Exports	9.45	10.00	-15.96	-14.76	48.49	42.00
	Imports	-4.96	-5.45	101.91	99.37	37.99	43.34
	Output	2.27	2.17	-13.43	-13.59	-8.40	-8.18
	Price	-1.56	-1.76	-5.35	-5.85	3.69	5.07
SUGAR	Exports	8.84	8.84	-54.51	-54.53	-6.29	-7.15
	Output	1.77	1.52	-1.93	-2.62	-2.62	-1.05
	Price	-1.56	-1.66	-2.16	-2.41	2.31	2.93
OTHER FOODS	Exports	1.95	1.43	10.73	9.28	27.75	31.66
	Imports	0.41	0.10	427.31	423.12	295.69	304.85
	Output	1.28	0.84	0.77	-0.39	-4.51	-1.73
	Price	-0.42	-0.40	-4.29	-4.23	-2.63	-2.76
TEXTILES	Output	1.06	0.42	2.82	1.12	-4.35	0.14
	Price	-0.21	-0.05	-0.37	0.07	0.09	-1.13
INTERMEDIATES	Output	0.67	0.07	2.04	0.45	-3.25	0.83
	Price	0.03	0.22	0.52	1.03	1.60	0.06
DURABLES	Output	0.65	0.04	2.05	0.43	-13.62	-9.82
	Price	0.12	0.25	1.17	1.51	-13.27	-14.27

Table 15. (end)

		In Agriculture				Economy-wide	
		1A		1B			
		1	2	1	2	1	2
VALUE ADDED	Agricultural	0.12	-0.46	-0.31	-1.76	6.60	10.29
	Non-agricultural	1.02	0.57	2.15	0.97	-7.00	-4.11
WAGES	Agricultural	0.07	0.53	-0.18	0.63	2.56	3.47
	Non-agricultural	-0.26	0.32	-0.95	0.57	0.72	-3.28
HOUSEHOLD	Landless	0.58	0.52	1.68	1.42	-1.57	-0.30
REAL INCOME	Small Farmer	0.51	0.26	1.24	0.57	-3.07	-1.33
	Medium Farmer	0.61	0.18	1.15	0.05	-1.44	1.06
	Large Farmer	0.63	0.09	1.02	-0.36	1.58	4.82
	Worker	1.01	0.69	2.53	1.69	-6.12	-4.12
	Marginal	1.24	0.84	2.95	1.90	-6.58	-4.11
	Capitalist	1.26	0.63	3.23	1.56	-7.35	-3.40

1. Wages adjust partially to food prices.
2. Full employment, labour supply elasticity of 0.3.

105

Table 16. Scenario 3: Liberalisation of World Agricultural Trade
(Changes from base-year levels, per cent)

		Scenario 3A		Scenario 3B		Scenario 3C	
		1	2	1	2	1	2
AGGREGATES	GDP	0.08	0.01	0.41	0.84	-4.09	0.51
	Investment	0.17	0.05	-3.11	-2.25	-6.71	-1.23
	Exports	2.91	2.81	8.83	9.64	53.58	62.22
	Imports	2.12	2.05	5.30	5.94	45.63	52.19
	Agricultural Exports	20.48	20.47	103.73	103.13	265.85	255.26
	Non-agric. Exports	-0.14	-0.25	-7.66	-6.60	16.71	28.68
	Agricultural Imports	19.47	19.47	65.25	66.75	29.11	40.35
	Non-agric. Imports	0.11	0.03	-1.63	-1.09	47.54	53.56
	Exchange Rate	-0.13	-0.13	-4.35	-4.15	16.14	17.65
	Government Revenue	0.15	0.08	-2.69	-2.15	-4.55	-2.61
	Government Savings	0.47	0.09	-16.65	-13.89	-26.03	-17.84
	Food Subsidy	0.04	-0.18	-8.90	-7.42	-9.45	2.42
	Fertilizer Subsidy	-0.04	-0.12	3.84	4.18	13.35	16.92
	Consumer Subsidy	2.00	1.48	52.49	55.09	120.27	144.97
	Total Subsidies	0.56	0.46	0.44	1.04	-1.88	2.51
	Terms of Trade	0.03	-0.09	3.85	4.58	10.51	17.20
RICE	Exports	...	...	1330.51	1310.51	2453.28	2233.70
	Imports	...	...	-44.68	-43.45	-78.69	-75.12
	Output	0.00	0.00	6.49	6.39	11.54	10.62
	Price	0.02	-0.06	10.87	11.30	24.25	27.57
WHEAT	Imports	...	...	-40.16	-38.80	-90.18	-84.80
	Output	-0.28	-0.28	1.35	1.31	1.55	1.83
	Price	0.65	0.57	5.78	6.18	13.98	18.68
COARSE CEREALS	Output	0.00	0.00	-0.75	-0.83	-2.10	-1.83
	Price	0.04	-0.04	3.53	4.30	6.77	10.99

Table 16. (continued)

		Scenario					
		3A		3B		3C	
		1	2	1	2	1	2
OTHER CROPS	Exports	...	...	5.46	5.16	20.83	16.80
	Imports	...	...	181.63	183.02	125.78	139.94
	Output	0.06	0.05	-2.65	-2.59	-4.72	-3.98
	Price	-0.12	-0.22	-1.60	-1.05	1.98	7.74
EDIBLE OILS	Exports	...	...	22.65	22.27	108.68	97.69
	Imports		...	54.17	54.75	5.93	11.65
	Output	-0.73	-0.75	-8.14	-8.13	-3.35	-3.04
	Price	2.24	2.19	-0.99	-0.69	7.68	10.46
SUGAR	Exports	...	...	-30.30	-29.92	38.77	40.45
	Output	0.83	0.80	-1.35	-1.12	0.10	2.55
	Price	-1.63	-1.66	-0.80	-0.67	3.69	4.87
OTHER FOODS	Exports	...	...	20.95	21.59	38.99	46.46
	Imports	...	...	359.06	359.54	245.88	255.11
	Output	0.96	0.92	-0.30	0.05	-5.09	-0.90
	Price	-1.28	-1.28	-4.41	-4.40	-3.25	-3.38
TEXTILES	Output	0.05	-0.03	-0.17	0.43	-8.61	-1.83
	Price	-0.03	-0.00	-0.63	-0.79	-0.78	-2.44
INTERMEDIATES	Output	0.08	-0.03	-1.43	-0.67	-7.33	-0.54
	Price	-0.02	0.00	-1.58	-1.69	-1.15	-3.05
DURABLES	Output	0.10	-0.02	-1.68	-0.85	-17.87	-11.33
	Price	-0.04	-0.02	-2.16	-2.20	-16.65	-17.72

Table 16. (end)

| | | Scenario | | | | | |
| | | 3A | | 3B | | 3C | |
		1	2	1	2	1	2
VALUE ADDED	Agricultural	-0.01	-0.12	4.88	5.43	13.24	19.26
	Non-agricultural	0.11	0.07	-1.29	-0.91	-10.68	-6.61
WAGES	Agricultural	0.02	-0.04	1.49	2.49	4.44	5.69
	Non-agricultural	-0.07	0.04	-0.06	-0.84	1.65	-5.18
HOUSEHOLD REAL INCOME	Landless	0.02	0.00	-1.19	-0.86	-4.51	-2.81
	Small Farmer	-0.02	-0.04	-0.50	-0.27	-4.47	-2.05
	Medium Farmer	0.05	-0.01	1.28	1.55	-0.59	3.03
	Large Farmer	0.02	-0.05	3.03	3.42	4.67	9.52
	Worker	0.16	0.14	-0.51	-0.32	-9.24	-6.54
	Marginal	0.15	0.12	-0.76	-0.51	-10.30	-6.96
	Capitalist	0.24	0.16	-0.87	-0.35	-11.43	-5.73

1. Wages adjust partially to food prices.
2. Full employment.

Table 17. **Scenario 4: 10 per cent Increase in Yields**
(Changes from base-year levels, per cent)

		Rice					Wheat	Coarse Cereals	Other Crops	All Crops
	4A[1]	4A[2]	4B[3]	4B1[4]	4B2[5]	4B3[6]	4C	4D	4E	4F
AGGREGATES										
GDP	1.23	0.38	1.32	1.05	0.89	1.09	0.57	0.18	4.69	6.81
Investment	5.09	3.17	6.09	3.40	2.00	0.69	2.57	0.92	11.98	20.93
Exports	3.55	1.86	4.20	3.46	3.06	1.74	-0.45	0.83	9.05	12.99
Imports	2.58	1.28	3.43	1.98	1.24	1.06	-0.53	0.68	6.74	9.46
Agricultural Exports	14.46	14.43	3.78	35.80	51.09	13.68	-1.50	1.13	22.81	37.08
Non-agric. Exports	1.66	-0.32	4.28	-2.16	-5.29	-0.33	-0.26	0.78	6.66	8.81
Agricultural Imports	-1.96	-3.98	0.78	1.22	1.48	0.31	-17.35	-0.12	-3.64	-24.91
Non-agric. Imports	3.10	1.89	3.74	2.06	1.21	1.15	1.42	0.78	7.94	13.43
Exchange Rate	0.28	-0.06	1.60	-1.64	-3.24	-0.45	-0.45	0.35	1.59	1.75
Government Revenue	2.74	1.55	3.47	1.56	0.57	1.31	1.08	0.71	7.71	12.43
Government Savings	22.59	16.17	27.03	15.03	8.89	2.67	11.85	4.02	44.77	84.72
Food Subsidy	-43.26	-44.46	-41.74	-45.42	-48.00	24.32	-33.14	-1.52	-4.92	-84.60
Fertilizer Subsidy	0.49	-0.30	0.69	0.78	1.25	0.48	0.25	2.80	-0.79	2.16
Consumer Subsidy	-41.85	-45.29	-47.76	-30.21	-19.50	-31.56	-25.61	0.12	7.22	-59.85
Total Subsidies	-7.43	-8.38	-7.46	-6.90	-6.75	6.51	-6.60	0.37	2.39	-11.66
Terms of Trade	-2.49	-3.35	-3.35	-1.18	-0.06	-1.65	-0.74	-1.05	-5.38	-9.53
RICE Exports	270.25	281.55	...	799.56	1199.34	304.61	-6.80	5.05	5.61	277.87
Imports	-83.27	-84.05	...	...	...	-85.80	11.20	-6.35	-4.40	-83.00
Output	7.70	7.69	6.29	9.55	11.26	9.20	-0.02	0.31	1.29	9.47
Price	-13.16	-13.72	-15.02	-10.31	-7.35	-9.83	0.26	-0.19	0.83	-12.27
WHEAT Imports	4.13	1.09	...	...	...	10.05	-51.05	-0.17	7.98	-42.32
Output	0.38	0.41	0.69	0.37	0.18	-0.03	9.84	0.17	1.17	11.87
Price	0.36	-0.18	0.41	1.15	1.52	0.17	-8.98	0.26	1.53	-6.72
COARSE CEREALS Output	0.76	0.53	1.01	0.40	0.08	0.48	0.11	5.25	1.20	7.57
Price	-0.93	-0.96	-1.81	0.30	1.37	-0.01	0.15	-15.12	0.35	-15.31

109

Table 17. (continued)

		4A¹	4A²	4B³	Rice 4B1⁴	Rice 4B2⁵	4B3⁶	Wheat 4C	Coarse Cereals 4D	Other Crops 4E	All Crops 4F
OTHER CROPS	Exports	0.41	0.93	...	...	...	-0.97	-0.82	0.36	24.64	24.51
	Imports	1.14	0.19	...	...	...	2.03	1.21	0.05	-7.93	-5.66
	Output	0.73	0.60	1.08	0.20	-0.27	0.35	0.08	0.22	8.93	10.04
	Price	0.60	-0.39	0.28	1.12	1.54	0.88	0.45	0.21	-11.25	-10.09
EDIBLE OILS	Exports	-0.21	0.42	5.04	-7.62	-13.46	-3.37	-2.48	0.64	44.46	41.39
	Imports	1.47	0.52	-2.09	6.94	11.74	3.52	2.27	-0.14	-17.10	-13.96
	Output	0.59	0.46	1.47	-0.76	-1.91	-0.06	-0.18	0.25	10.12	10.86
	Price	0.50	-0.05	0.67	0.25	0.02	0.45	0.17	0.24	-5.69	-4.78
SUGAR	Exports	-0.16	-0.82	6.07	-8.80	-15.50	-3.91	-2.74	0.78	40.27	37.14
	Output	0.73	0.29	1.28	-0.07	-0.72	0.32	0.01	0.27	8.19	9.18
	Price	0.52	0.24	0.35	0.80	1.02	0.71	0.30	0.21	-5.36	-4.37
OTHER FOODS	Exports	1.19	0.13	2.98	-1.50	-3.73	-0.10	0.07	0.67	8.61	10.55
	Imports	1.83	1.46	0.76	3.35	4.63	2.15	1.14	0.18	4.06	7.29
	Output	1.46	0.71	1.97	0.62	-0.09	0.88	0.54	0.45	6.51	9.01
	Price	0.56	0.54	0.57	0.57	0.56	0.58	0.04	0.12	-0.46	0.28
TEXTILES	Output	1.14	0.02	1.50	0.58	0.08	0.78	0.32	0.29	4.77	6.55
	Price	0.58	0.78	0.67	0.44	0.31	0.53	0.19	0.23	0.53	1.55
INTERMEDIATES	Output	2.04	0.61	2.62	1.09	0.29	0.57	0.89	0.42	5.46	8.79
	Price	0.80	0.91	1.23	0.16	-0.39	0.22	0.24	0.31	2.11	3.46
DURABLES	Output	2.38	0.79	3.03	1.33	0.45	0.46	1.10	0.43	6.05	9.93
	Price	0.84	0.83	1.46	-0.09	-0.87	0.10	0.18	0.33	2.40	3.74

Table 17. (end)

		Rice						Wheat	Coarse Cereals	Other Crops	All Crops
		4A[1]	4A[2]	4B[3]	4B1[4]	4B2[5]	4B3[6]	4C	4D	4E	4F
VALUE ADDED	Agricultural	-0.90	-1.99	-2.06	0.85	2.34	0.18	0.40	-0.85	-1.53	-2.98
	Non-agricultural	2.04	1.28	2.61	1.13	0.34	1.43	0.63	0.60	7.05	10.53
WAGES	Agricultural	-1.76	-0.33	-2.13	-1.17	-0.61	-1.18	-0.35	-1.00	-1.26	-4.25
	Non-agricultural	-0.41	0.89	-0.54	-0.17	0.04	-0.19	-0.17	0.01	-1.26	-1.80
HOUSEHOLD	Landless	2.27	2.38	2.74	1.50	0.80	1.70	0.57	0.66	3.97	7.75
REAL INCOME	Small Farmer	2.68	2.35	2.93	2.23	1.77	2.20	0.77	1.01	4.05	8.85
	Medium Farmer	1.68	0.94	1.47	1.90	2.03	1.64	0.81	0.59	3.27	6.58
	Large Farmer	0.44	-0.51	-0.17	1.30	2.00	0.84	0.57	-0.06	1.78	2.83
	Worker	1.43	0.92	1.89	0.69	0.05	0.73	0.49	0.32	5.59	7.91
	Marginal	1.76	1.14	2.32	0.85	0.06	1.30	0.46	0.49	7.21	10.12
	Capitalist	2.24	1.10	2.90	1.16	0.25	1.23	0.86	0.57	7.68	11.50

1. Wages adjust partially to food prices.
2. Full employment.
3. Agricultural trade is fixed.
4. Rice exports increase by 4 per cent of base-year output.
5. Rice exports increase by 6 per cent of base-year output.
6. Rice procurement increases 20 per cent.

111

Table 18. **Scenario 5: 80 per cent Reduction in Fertilizer Subsidy**

(Changes from base-year levels, per cent)

		Scenario		
		5B[1]	5B[2]	5C[3]
AGGREGATES	GDP	-0.50	-0.33	-0.52
	Investment	0.86	1.21	0.83
	Exports	-0.21	0.12	-0.22
	Imports	-0.08	0.17	-0.09
	Agricultural Exports	-1.09	-1.06	-1.12
	Non-agricultural Exports	-0.06	0.33	-0.06
	Agricultural Imports	1.60	2.13	1.63
	Non-agricultural Imports	-0.28	-0.05	-0.29
	Exchange Rate	0.05	0.11	0.06
	Government Revenue	-0.44	-0.22	-0.45
	Government Savings	7.49	8.65	7.38
	Food Subsidy	4.14	4.55	4.35
	Fertilizer Subsidy	-83.06	-83.04	-83.01
	Consumer Subsidy	2.80	3.67	2.92
	Total Subsidies	-12.58	-12.38	-12.54
	Terms of Trade	0.29	0.52	0.30
RICE	Exports	-2.11	-3.13	-2.11
	Imports	2.47	4.10	2.43
	Output	-0.27	-0.27	-0.28
	Price	0.31	0.47	0.32
WHEAT	Imports	2.89	3.63	2.97
	Output	-0.82	-0.83	-0.86
	Price	0.61	0.72	0.64

Table 18. (continued)

		Scenario		
		5B[1]	5B[2]	5C[3]
COARSE CEREALS	Output	0.69	0.69	0.73
	Price	-2.78	-2.62	-2.95
OTHER CROPS	Exports	-1.32	-1.44	-1.38
	Imports	0.28	0.48	0.27
	Output	-0.61	-0.59	-0.64
	Price	0.78	0.97	0.81
EDIBLE OILS	Exports	-2.02	-2.16	-2.08
	Imports	0.83	1.03	0.84
	Output	-0.62	-0.60	-0.65
	Price	0.43	0.53	0.44
FERTILIZER	Imports	-16.64	-16.72	-14.00
	Output	-12.15	-12.01	-13.03
	Consumption	-10.43	-10.43	-10.97
	Price	17.83	17.83	18.94
	Producer price	-5.78	-5.78	-4.84
	Value added	-43.34	-43.08	-40.12

Table 18. (end)

		Scenario	
	5B[1]	5B[2]	5C[3]
VALUE ADDED			
Agricultural	-0.30	-0.08	-0.33
Non-agricultural	-0.57	-0.42	-0.60
HOUSEHOLD			
REAL INCOME			
Landless	-0.18	-0.13	-0.19
Small Farmer	-0.31	-0.23	-0.33
Medium Farmer	-0.44	-0.31	-0.46
Large Farmer	-0.47	-0.29	-0.49
Worker	-0.36	-0.27	-0.39
Marginal	-0.46	-0.35	-0.49
Capitalist	-0.96	-0.75	-0.92

1. Elasticity of capital-labour substitution for fertilizer is 0.8, wage adjusts to food prices.
2. Elasticity of capital-labour substitution for fertilizer is 0.8, full employment.
3. Elasticity of capital-labour substitution for fertilizer is 1.1, wage adjusts to food prices.

114

Table 19. **Scenarios 6 and 7: Food Subsidy Policy**
(Changes from base-year levels, per cent)

		Scenario[1]				
		6A	6B1	6B2	6B3	7
AGGREGATES	GDP	0.20	-0.10	0.04	-0.01	0.01
	Investment	-0.29	-0.00	-0.23	0.01	-0.44
	Exports	-0.28	-0.35	-0.49	0.01	-0.02
	Imports	-0.31	-0.31	-0.46	0.01	0.00
	Agricultural Exports	0.55	-0.04	-0.26	0.02	-0.56
	Non-agricultural Exports	-0.42	-0.40	-0.53	0.01	0.07
	Agricultural Imports	0.69	-3.61	-3.56	0.00	1.97
	Non-agricultural Imports	-0.42	0.08	-0.10	0.01	-0.22
	Exchange Rate	-0.33	-0.19	-0.28	0.01	0.02
	Government Revenue	-2.04	0.91	0.91	0.11	-0.22
	Government Savings	...	...	...	...	-1.47
	Food Subsidy	-77.09	32.55	32.51	3.78	0.69
	Fertilizer Subsidy	0.72	-0.11	0.05	-0.02	0.18
	Consumer Subsidy	-100.00	7.58	7.34	7.56	2.52
	Total Subsidies	-15.30	6.82	6.82	0.81	0.16
	Terms of Trade	0.79	-0.01	0.01	0.00	0.46
RICE	Exports	33.09	9.76	8.86	0.06	-5.21
	Imports	-7.82	-14.60	-13.54	-0.10	8.79
	Output	0.88	0.04	0.03	-0.00	0.11
	Price	2.59	0.24	0.23	0.00	0.54
WHEAT	Imports	3.46	-7.96	-7.60	-0.04	3.50
	Output	-0.16	0.30	0.28	0.00	-0.03
	Price	0.32	0.66	0.60	0.01	0.25

Table 19. (end)

		Scenario[1]				
		6A	6B1	6B2	6B3	7
COARSE CEREALS	Output	-0.19	-0.01	-0.02	-0.00	0.16
	Price	0.73	-0.05	-0.01	-0.00	0.62
OTHER CROPS	Exports	-0.89	-0.18	-0.26	0.00	-0.33
	Imports	0.56	0.04	0.19	-0.01	0.36
	Output	-0.24	-0.08	-0.06	-0.00	-0.02
	Price	0.32	-0.09	-0.08	0.00	0.33
EDIBLE OILS	Exports	-1.44	-0.68	-0.81	-0.00	-0.68
	Imports	0.28	0.70	0.52	0.04	0.37
	Output	-0.19	-0.23	-0.16	-0.01	-0.17
	Price	-0.21	0.06	-0.11	0.02	0.16
SUGAR	Exports	-1.61	-0.69	-1.05	0.02	-0.35
	Output	-0.08	-0.16	-0.10	-0.01	0.11
	Price	-0.17	0.10	-0.03	0.02	0.15
OTHER FOODS	Exports	-0.47	-0.40	-0.40	0.00	-0.27
	Imports	-0.32	0.13	0.16	0.02	-0.38
	Output	-0.30	-0.23	-0.15	0.00	-0.32
	Price	-0.35	0.12	-0.02	0.02	-0.02
HOUSEHOLD	Landless	-0.20	-0.19	-0.05	-0.02	1.57
REAL INCOME	Small Farmer	-0.11	-0.18	-0.03	-0.02	1.77
	Medium Farmer	0.27	-0.18	-0.01	-0.02	0.09
	Large Farmer	0.67	-0.17	-0.80	-0.02	0.26
	Worker	-0.45	-0.22	0.05	0.01	-0.80
	Marginal	-1.45	-0.08	0.18	0.07	-0.66
	Capitalist	0.21	-0.29	-1.11	-0.04	-0.19

1. All scenarios are with full employment.

MAIN SALES OUTLETS OF OECD PUBLICATIONS
PRINCIPAUX POINTS DE VENTE DES PUBLICATIONS DE L'OCDE

ARGENTINA – ARGENTINE
Carlos Hirsch S.R.L.
Galería Güemes, Florida 165, 4° Piso
1333 Buenos Aires   Tel. (1) 331.1787 y 331.2391
Telefax: (1) 331.1787

AUSTRALIA – AUSTRALIE
D.A. Information Services
648 Whitehorse Road, P.O.B 163
Mitcham, Victoria 3132   Tel. (03) 873.4411
Telefax: (03) 873.5679

AUSTRIA – AUTRICHE
Gerold & Co.
Graben 31
Wien I   Tel. (0222) 533.50.14

BELGIUM – BELGIQUE
Jean De Lannoy
Avenue du Roi 202
B-1060 Bruxelles   Tel. (02) 538.51.69/538.08.41
Telefax: (02) 538.08.41

CANADA
Renouf Publishing Company Ltd.
1294 Algoma Road
Ottawa, ON K1B 3W8   Tel. (613) 741.4333
Telefax: (613) 741.5439
Stores:
61 Sparks Street
Ottawa, ON K1P 5R1   Tel. (613) 238.8985
211 Yonge Street
Toronto, ON M5B 1M4   Tel. (416) 363.3171

Les Éditions La Liberté Inc.
3020 Chemin Sainte-Foy
Sainte-Foy, PQ G1X 3V6   Tel. (418) 658.3763
Telefax: (418) 658.3763

Federal Publications
165 University Avenue
Toronto, ON M5H 3B8   Tel. (416) 581.1552
Telefax: (416) 581.1743

Les Publications Fédérales
1185 Avenue de l'Université
Montréal, PQ H3B 3A7   Tel. (514) 954.1633
Telefax : (514) 954.1633

CHINA – CHINE
China National Publications Import
Export Corporation (CNPIEC)
16 Gongti E. Road, Chaoyang District
P.O. Box 88 or 50
Beijing 100704 PR   Tel. (01) 506.6688
Telefax: (01) 506.3101

DENMARK – DANEMARK
Munksgaard Export and Subscription Service
35, Nørre Søgade, P.O. Box 2148
DK-1016 København K   Tel. (33) 12.85.70
Telefax: (33) 12.93.87

FINLAND – FINLANDE
Akateeminen Kirjakauppa
Keskuskatu 1, P.O. Box 128
00100 Helsinki   Tel. (358 0) 12141
Telefax: (358 0) 121.4441

FRANCE
OECD/OCDE
Mail Orders/Commandes par correspondance:
2, rue André-Pascal
75775 Paris Cedex 16   Tel. (33-1) 45.24.82.00
Telefax: (33-1) 45.24.81.76   or (33-1) 45.24.85.00
Telex: 640048 OCDE

OECD Bookshop/Librairie de l'OCDE :
33, rue Octave-Feuillet
75016 Paris   Tel. (33-1) 45.24.81.67
(33-1) 45.24.81.81

Documentation Française
29, quai Voltaire
75007 Paris   Tel. 40.15.70.00
Gibert Jeune (Droit-Économie)
6, place Saint-Michel
75006 Paris   Tel. 43.25.91.19
Librairie du Commerce International
10, avenue d'Iéna
75016 Paris   Tel. 40.73.34.60
Librairie Dunod
Université Paris-Dauphine
Place du Maréchal de Lattre de Tassigny
75016 Paris   Tel. 47.27.18.56
Librairie Lavoisier
11, rue Lavoisier
75008 Paris   Tel. 42.65.39.95
Librairie L.G.D.J. - Montchrestien
20, rue Soufflot
75005 Paris   Tel. 46.33.89.85
Librairie des Sciences Politiques
30, rue Saint-Guillaume
75007 Paris   Tel. 45.48.36.02
P.U.F.
49, boulevard Saint-Michel
75005 Paris   Tel. 43.25.83.40
Librairie de l'Université
12a, rue Nazareth
13100 Aix-en-Provence   Tel. (16) 42.26.18.08
Documentation Française
165, rue Garibaldi
69003 Lyon   Tel. (16) 78.63.32.23
Librairie Decitre
29, place Bellecour
69002 Lyon   Tel. (16) 72.40.54.54

GERMANY – ALLEMAGNE
OECD Publications and Information Centre
August-Bebel-Allee 6
D-W 5300 Bonn 2   Tel. (0228) 959.120
Telefax: (0228) 959.12.17

GREECE – GRÈCE
Librairie Kauffmann
Mavrokordatou 9
106 78 Athens   Tel. 322.21.60
Telefax: 363.39.67

HONG-KONG
Swindon Book Co. Ltd.
13–15 Lock Road
Kowloon, Hong Kong   Tel. 366.80.31
Telefax: 739.49.75

HUNGARY – HONGRIE
Euro Info Service
kázmér u.45
1121 Budapest   Tel. (1) 182.00.44
Telefax : (1) 182.00.44

ICELAND – ISLANDE
Mál Mog Menning
Laugavegi 18, Pósthólf 392
121 Reykjavik   Tel. 162.35.23

INDIA – INDE
Oxford Book and Stationery Co.
Scindia House
New Delhi 110001   Tel.(11) 331.5896/5308
Telefax: (11) 332.5993
17 Park Street
Calcutta 700016   Tel. 240832

INDONESIA – INDONÉSIE
Pdii-Lipi
P.O. Box 269/JKSMG/88
Jakarta 12790   Tel. 583467
Telex: 62 875

IRELAND – IRLANDE
TDC Publishers – Library Suppliers
12 North Frederick Street
Dublin 1   Tel. 74.48.35/74.96.77
Telefax: 74.84.16

ISRAEL
Electronic Publications only
Publications électroniques seulement
Sophist Systems Ltd.
71 Allenby Street
Tel-Aviv 65134   Tel. 3-29.00.21
Telefax: 3-29.92.39

ITALY – ITALIE
Libreria Commissionaria Sansoni
Via Duca di Calabria 1/1
50125 Firenze   Tel. (055) 64.54.15
Telefax: (055) 64.12.57
Via Bartolini 29
20155 Milano   Tel. (02) 36.50.83
Editrice e Libreria Herder
Piazza Montecitorio 120
00186 Roma   Tel. 679.46.28
Telefax: 678.47.51
Libreria Hoepli
Via Hoepli 5
20121 Milano   Tel. (02) 86.54.46
Telefax: (02) 805.28.86
Libreria Scientifica
Dott. Lucio de Biasio 'Aeiou'
Via Coronelli, 6
20146 Milano   Tel. (02) 48.95.45.52
Telefax: (02) 48.95.45.48

JAPAN – JAPON
OECD Publications and Information Centre
Landic Akasaka Building
2-3-4 Akasaka, Minato-ku
Tokyo 107   Tel. (81.3) 3586.2016
Telefax: (81.3) 3584.7929

KOREA – CORÉE
Kyobo Book Centre Co. Ltd.
P.O. Box 1658, Kwang Hwa Moon
Seoul   Tel. 730.78.91
Telefax: 735.00.30

MALAYSIA – MALAISIE
Co-operative Bookshop Ltd.
University of Malaya
P.O. Box 1127, Jalan Pantai Baru
59700 Kuala Lumpur
Malaysia   Tel. 756.5000/756.5425
Telefax: 757.3661

MEXICO – MEXIQUE
Revistas y Periodicos Internacionales S.A. de C.V.
Florencia 57 - 1004
Mexico, D.F. 06600   Tel. 207.81.00
Telefax : 208.39.79

NETHERLANDS – PAYS-BAS
SDU Uitgeverij
Christoffel Plantijnstraat 2
Postbus 20014
2500 EA's-Gravenhage   Tel. (070 3) 78.99.11
Voor bestellingen: Tel. (070 3) 78.98.80
Telefax: (070 3) 47.63.51

NEW ZEALAND
NOUVELLE-ZÉLANDE
Legislation Services
P.O. Box 12418
Thorndon, Wellington   Tel. (04) 496.5652
Telefax: (04) 496.5698

NORWAY – NORVÈGE
Narvesen Info Center – NIC
Bertrand Narvesens vei 2
P.O. Box 6125 Etterstad
0602 Oslo 6   Tel. (02) 57.33.00
                              Telefax: (02) 68.19.01

PAKISTAN
Mirza Book Agency
65 Shahrah Quaid-E-Azam
Lahore 54000   Tel. (42) 353.601
                              Telefax: (42) 231.730

PHILIPPINE – PHILIPPINES
International Book Center
5th Floor, Filipinas Life Bldg.
Ayala Avenue
Metro Manila   Tel. 81.96.76
                              Telex 23312 RHP PH

PORTUGAL
Livraria Portugal
Rua do Carmo 70-74
Apart. 2681
1117 Lisboa Codex   Tel.: (01) 347.49.82/3/4/5
                              Telefax: (01) 347.02.64

SINGAPORE – SINGAPOUR
Information Publications Pte. Ltd.
41, Kallang Pudding, No. 04-03
Singapore 1334   Tel. 741.5166
                              Telefax: 742.9356

SPAIN – ESPAGNE
Mundi-Prensa Libros S.A.
Castelló 37, Apartado 1223
Madrid 28001   Tel. (91) 431.33.99
                              Telefax: (91) 575.39.98

Librería Internacional AEDOS
Consejo de Ciento 391
08009 – Barcelona   Tel. (93) 488.34.92
                              Telefax: (93) 487.76.59
Llibreria de la Generalitat
Palau Moja
Rambla dels Estudis, 118
08002 – Barcelona
               (Subscripcions) Tel. (93) 318.80.12
               (Publicacions) Tel. (93) 302.67.23
                              Telefax: (93) 412.18.54

SRI LANKA
Centre for Policy Research
c/o Colombo Agencies Ltd.
No. 300-304, Galle Road
Colombo 3   Tel. (1) 574240, 573551-2
                              Telefax: (1) 575394, 510711

SWEDEN – SUÈDE
Fritzes Fackboksföretaget
Box 16356
Regeringsgatan 12
103 27 Stockholm   Tel. (08) 690.90.90
                              Telefax: (08) 20.50.21
Subscription Agency-Agence d'abonnements
Wennergren-Williams AB
P.O. Box 1305
171 25 Solna   Tél. (08) 705.97.50
                              Téléfax : (08) 27.00.71

SWITZERLAND – SUISSE
Maditec S.A. (Books and Periodicals - Livres
et périodiques)
Chemin des Palettes 4
Case postale 2066
1020 Renens 1   Tel. (021) 635.08.65
                              Telefax: (021) 635.07.80

Librairie Payot S.A.
4, place Pépinet
1003 Lausanne   Tel. (021) 341.33.48
                              Telefax: (021) 341.33.45

Librairie Unilivres
6, rue de Candolle
1205 Genève   Tel. (022) 320.26.23
                              Telefax: (022) 329.73.18

Subscription Agency - Agence d'abonnement
Dynapresse Marketing S.A.
38 avenue Vibert
1227 Carouge   Tel.: (022) 308.07.89
                              Telefax : (022) 308.07.99

See also – Voir aussi :
OECD Publications and Information Centre
August-Bebel-Allee 6
D-W 5300 Bonn 2 (Germany) Tel. (0228) 959.120
                              Telefax: (0228) 959.12.17

TAIWAN – FORMOSE
Good Faith Worldwide Int'l. Co. Ltd.
9th Floor, No. 118, Sec. 2
Chung Hsiao E. Road
Taipei   Tel. (02) 391.7396/391.7397
                              Telefax: (02) 394.9176

THAILAND – THAÏLANDE
Suksit Siam Co. Ltd.
113, 115 Fuang Nakhon Rd.
Opp. Wat Rajbopith
Bangkok 10200   Tel. (662) 251.1630
                              Telefax: (662) 236.7783

TURKEY – TURQUIE
Kültür Yayinlari Is-Türk Ltd. Sti.
Atatürk Bulvari No. 191/Kat 13
Kavaklidere/Ankara   Tel. 428.11.40 Ext. 2458
Dolmabahce Cad. No. 29
Besiktas/Istanbul   Tel. 260.71.88
                              Telex: 43482B

UNITED KINGDOM – ROYAUME-UNI
HMSO
Gen. enquiries   Tel. (071) 873 0011
Postal orders only:
P.O. Box 276, London SW8 5DT
Personal Callers HMSO Bookshop
49 High Holborn, London WC1V 6HB
                              Telefax: (071) 873 8200
Branches at: Belfast, Birmingham, Bristol, Edin-
burgh, Manchester

UNITED STATES – ÉTATS-UNIS
OECD Publications and Information Centre
2001 L Street N.W., Suite 700
Washington, D.C. 20036-4910 Tel. (202) 785.6323
                              Telefax: (202) 785.0350

VENEZUELA
Libreria del Este
Avda F. Miranda 52, Aptdo. 60337
Edificio Galipán
Caracas 106   Tel. 951.1705/951.2307/951.1297
                      Telegram: Libreste Caracas

Subscription to OECD periodicals may also be
placed through main subscription agencies.

Les abonnements aux publications périodiques de
l'OCDE peuvent être souscrits auprès des
principales agences d'abonnement.

Orders and inquiries from countries where Distribu-
tors have not yet been appointed should be sent to:
OECD Publications Service, 2 rue André-Pascal,
75775 Paris Cedex 16, France.

Les commandes provenant de pays où l'OCDE n'a
pas encore désigné de distributeur devraient être
adressées à : OCDE, Service des Publications,
2, rue André-Pascal, 75775 Paris Cedex 16, France.

                                      02-1993

OECD PUBLICATIONS, 2 rue André-Pascal, 75775 PARIS CEDEX 16
PRINTED IN FRANCE
(41 93 03 1) ISBN 92-64-13851-X - No. 46545 1993

DO ███ CIRCULATE